MARRIED F

G000153640

MARRIED PRIESTS?

Thirty Crucial Questions about Celibacy

Edited by Arturo Cattaneo

together with
Manfred Hauke, André-Marie Jerumanis,
and Ernesto William Volonté

Foreword by
Cardinal Mauro Piacenza
Prefect of the Congregation for the Clergy

Translated by Michael J. Miller

IGNATIUS PRESS   SAN FRANCISCO

Original Italian edition:
Preti sposati? 30 domande scottanti sul celibato
© 2011 by Editrice Elledici, Rivoli, Italy

Cover photograph:
Priestly ordinations at Saint Peter's Basilica, Rome
© Stefano Spaziani

Cover design by Roxanne Mei Lum

© 2012 by Ignatius Press, San Francisco
All rights reserved
ISBN: 978-1-58617-725-6
Library of Congress Control Number 2012933890
Printed in the United States of America ∞

Contents

WHAT THEOLOGY SAYS ON THE SUBJECT

EMOTIONS AND SEXUALITY

PAPAL TEACHINGS ON THE SUBJECT FROM
PIUS XI TO BENEDICT XVI
By His Eminence Cardinal Mauro Piacenza

APPENDIX

Foreword

One of the criteria for evaluating the historical and faith consciousness of a particular epoch consists of the ability to distinguish between true and false, between good and evil and also between what is a gift and what is not. Ecclesiastical celibacy, *apostolica vivendi forma* [the apostolic way life], should be reckoned as one of the greatest goods and most powerful vehicles of truth, one of the greatest gifts that the Lord left to his Church and continually reaffirms.

These aspects of good, truth and gift must be kept in mind in order to understand the historical-theological and normative-spiritual reality of ecclesiastical celibacy, which is still able to foster a deepening of everyone's faith and to verify its quality and, above all, to encourage thinking as God does and not according to the ways of the world.

The Church, the Bride of the Lord, does not renounce the gifts of her Spouse, and in a continuous authentic renewal she implores the light and power of the Spirit, which enables her members to understand once again, to study and to live with ever greater fidelity the gift of celibacy.

If it is necessary to speak about reform—and personally I have thought for the last thirty years that it is—it must be understood, obviously, in an authentically Catholic sense; in other words, it must embrace the whole life of priests, along the lines of a radical fidelity to their proper identity, which plainly has not changed and cannot be modeled on the transient standards of the world, but rather requires them to conform themselves continuously to the will of God. Authentic reform cannot look solely to the psychological and emotional aspects of the life of a priest, but requires the courage to start again from the roots: a correct Christology, a sound ecclesiology, a robust spirituality and, above all, a correct sacramental theology and a profound sense of the sacred that is capable of shaping all of priestly life around the indispensable center, which is the celebration of the Eucharist. How do priests celebrate? What sense of the sacred do they convey? Are they clearly convinced of the absolute necessity of Christ for salvation? Only by answering these questions will it be possible to understand again sacred celibacy authentically and to be enthusiastically committed to it, whereas without this broad context of genuine faith it could become absolutely incomprehensible.

Over the centuries—and this dynamic has been evident in recent decades as well—there have been plenty of attacks on ecclesiastical celibacy. It is necessary to recognize that not infrequently they come from contexts and mindsets that are completely foreign to the faith, understood both as doctrine and practice, and, unfortunately, are often orchestrated by interest groups that do not even disguise the fact that their goal is the gradual weakening of one of the elements that makes witness to Christ more effective: virginity for the sake of the kingdom of heaven.

Celibacy is no more foreign to contemporary culture than marital fidelity or premarital continence might seem to be. We must recognize that we are faced with one of the greatest educational challenges of the modern era; ever since the 1968 revolution, which promised the liberation of man but in reality made him a slave to his own instincts, it is urgently necessary to reeducate the whole emotional sphere, acknowledging its greatness and dignity but at the same time placing it within the framework of objective limitations that theology calls original sin, with the consequences that result from it.

The underlying logic of priestly celibacy is the same one we may encounter in Christian matrimony: the total gift of everything forever in love. Behind the dynamic of self-giving on the part of the priest is the primacy of God and, consequently, also the primacy of his will, which freely calls those whom he wants.

Last but not least, it is necessary to emphasize the connection between difficulties in understanding the value of ecclesiastical celibacy and the widespread semi-Pelagian culture, because of which contemporary man, the victim of his own scientific technology, thinks that he can accomplish something good without the help of grace. The ingenuous optimism about the world found even in some theological and ecclesiastical circles is not immune to that risk and requires deep discernment and a sound, constructively critical mind. In the course of its now bimillennial history, in times of great trial, crisis and scandal, the Church has never lowered her moral and spiritual standards but, on the contrary, has held them high and even raised them, above all in the very delicate task of selecting, educating and appointing her own ministers.

Benedict XVI reminded priests on March 16, 2009, that "no one proclaims himself in the first person, but within and through his own humanity every priest must be well aware that he is bringing to the world Another, God himself. God is the only treasure which ultimately people desire to find in a priest."

The priestly model is that of the witness to the Absolute. The real contradiction today is not to seek superficial originality, which stirs up short-lived interest. Priests will truly be a "sign of contradiction" only insofar as they become holy while fully living out their own specific identity. There is no other way!

Let us look, for example, to Saint John-Mary Vianney, Saint John Bosco, Saint Maximilian Kolbe, Saint Pio of Pietrelcina, Saint Josemaría Escrivá and so many others— all of them priests, all extremely different in their human personality and personal history and yet all extraordinarily united by their love for and witness to Christ our Lord and by having been, by that very fact, truly prophetic signs.

The fact that celibacy is little understood or appreciated today in many circles must not lead us to speculate about different scenarios, but rather requires an effort to promote more careful, ongoing formation of priests as well as better catechesis of the lay faithful. We pastors must not betray the youth by lowering the requirements but must preserve their aspirations by encouraging them to strive for the heights. In order to do that we cannot fear the world or be influenced by it in any way. We must ardently follow the Spirit of God, act resolutely as though everything depended on us, but with the patience and interior peace of someone who knows that everything depends on God, and place all our efforts into the hands of the Immaculate Virgin, the splendid Icon of fidelity to her Lord and ours!

Therefore I can only hope that this book will find the widest possible readership, thus contributing to an ever greater appreciation of priestly celibacy as a precious gift of the Spirit of Christ to his Church and received by young men who—like Saint Paul and so many saints—allow themselves to be "won over by Christ" (cf. Phil 3:12).

His Eminence Cardinal Mauro Piacenza
Prefect of the Congregation for the Clergy

To Whom This Book Is Addressed

With this book we wish to make comprehensible to the general public the reasons the Church has priestly celibacy so much at heart. For this purpose a response is given to the most frequent and most critical questions regarding priestly celibacy, grouped according to various topics. To facilitate reading, the responses are deliberately concise. A collection of excerpts from the principal documents of the Magisterium and a bibliography that allows for the possibility of more in-depth reading are included at the end of this volume

The growing shortage of priests in almost all the Western world, the abandonment of the ministry by priests who get married and the scandals caused by acts of sexual abuse have given new relevance to the question of whether it might not be better for the Church to abandon the celibacy requirement for her ministers. Apropos it is also asserted that priestly celibacy is not a matter of dogma but only of discipline and that, as such, it could therefore be modified so as to allow the priestly ordination of married men. Some lay faithful are therefore perplexed and have a hard time understanding why the Church continues to reaffirm its importance.

Many of the critiques of priestly celibacy come from those who see the priesthood simply as a form of social service and do not acknowledge its supernatural role. Anyone who sees the priest merely as someone who organizes the community of believers, presides at liturgical celebrations or offers spiritual advice of the take-out variety will grant the importance of the respective competences but will not be able to appreciate the value of celibacy. It must be remembered that the mystery of the Church cannot be reduced to secular categories. The Church is in the world but not of the world.

The questions answered here are very heterogeneous, and consequently the answers mention a wide variety of considerations too. If one wanted, however, to identify the nucleus of the reasons that have brought the Church—guided by the Holy Spirit—to acquire a consciousness of the manifold and important reasons in favor of celibacy, the first thing that must be remembered is the example of the life of Christ. This exampled has illuminated the life of the Church from the first centuries, as historical research testifies: at the beginning, from the moment of ordination, a pledge of continence (or abstinence) was required; later on the Church tended to require a promise of celibacy.

Besides the exemplary model offered by Christ to his priests, we should recall the luminous witness of countless holy priests who have followed the example of Jesus precisely by devoting themselves fully to his service and to the service of all souls. Hence it is possible to declare that the Church, while progressing in her understanding of the salvific plan of God manifested in Christ, progressed also in her understanding of the importance of the priesthood-celibacy connection.

With ever greater clarity the Magisterium of the Church has identified the theological reason for priestly celibacy as the configuration of the priest to Jesus Christ, the Head and Bridegroom of the Church. This is how the apostolic exhortation *Pastores Dabo Vobis* (1992), for example, put it: "The Church, as the Spouse of Jesus Christ, wishes to be loved by the priest in the total and exclusive manner in which Jesus Christ her Head and Spouse loved her. Priestly celibacy, then, is the gift of self in and with Christ to his Church and expresses the priest's service to the Church in and with the Lord" (no. 29). The biblical, theological and spiritual perspective that associates the ministerial priesthood with that of Christ and considers his total and exclusive dedication to his saving mission exemplary is so profound and richly consequential that the encyclical of Paul VI on celibacy invites all "to go deeply into the inner recesses and wealth of its reality. In this way, the bond between the priesthood and celibacy will more and more be seen as closely knit" (no. 25). This reasoning allows the priest to consider and to practice celibacy not as an isolated or purely negative element (difficult renunciation), but in a supremely positive sense, that is, as the fruit of a free, loving choice—which is to be renewed continually—in response to an invitation from God to follow Christ in his gift of self as "Spouse of the Church", thus participating in the fatherhood and the fruitfulness of God.

It is not difficult to understand why these profound theological reasons in favor of priestly celibacy cannot be undermined in the least by the lack of priestly vocations, by the number of failed vocations or by the seriously scandalous behaviors—which are absolutely deplorable—on the part of some priests. It would be as if someone demanded that the indissolubility of marriage be abolished based on an increase in marital infidelity or divorce. What must be recognized instead is that many emotional crises in priestly life are caused mainly by the lack of strong experiences of that spiritual fatherhood that prompted Saint Paul to exclaim, "I became your father in Christ Jesus" (1 Cor 4:15), and to turn to the faithful, calling them "my little children, with whom I am again in travail" (Gal 4:19).

Some people reproach the Church for trying to impose by law something that ought to be a free choice. It is easy to see, however, that this argument is bogus, since celibacy is imposed neither by Christ nor by the Church. The latter limits herself to choosing candidates for priestly ministry from among those who—together with other requirements—have received the gift of celibacy. But in order for this gift to continue to be resplendent and fruitful, the priest must renew each day his gift of self to God, to the Church and to souls, thus transforming his life into a joyous affirmation of love.

Just before the inauguration of the Year for Priests, on June 15–16, 2009, a meeting took place between Pope Benedict XVI and several representatives of the Catholic Church in Austria; to that meeting Cardinal Christoph Schönborn brought a petition from Austrian Catholics calling for (among other things) the abolition of the celibacy requirement for priests. According to a later report by the same cardinal, the pope reacted by forcefully reaffirming the importance of priestly celibacy: "The Holy Father said that the question, basically, is whether we think that it is possible and makes sense to live a life founded solely and uniquely on God."

The pope summarized a reflection that he had already offered on December 22, 2006, in an address to the Roman Curia:

> The true foundation of celibacy can be contained in the phrase: *Dominus pars*—You are my land.[1] It can only be theocentric. It cannot mean being deprived of love, but must

[1] The full verse quoted earlier in the address is Psalm 16[15]:5: *"Dominus pars hereditatis meae et calicis mei."* ("The Lord is my chosen portion and my cup.") For a fuller explanation, see the entire address by the Holy Father in the appendix.

mean letting oneself be consumed by passion for God and subsequently, thanks to a more intimate way of being with him, to serve men and women, too. Celibacy must be a witness to faith: faith in God materializes in that form of life which only has meaning if it is based on God. Basing one's life on him, renouncing marriage and the family, means that I accept and experience God as a reality and that I can therefore bring him to men and women.... This theocentricity of the priestly existence is truly necessary in our entirely function-oriented world in which everything is based on calculable and ascertainable performance. The priest must truly know God from within and thus bring him to men and women: this is the prime service that contemporary humanity needs. If this centrality of God in a priest's life is lost, little by little the zeal in his actions is lost. In an excess of external things the centre that gives meaning to all things and leads them back to unity is missing. There, the foundation of life, the 'land' upon which all this can stand and prosper, is missing. Celibacy, in force for Bishops throughout the Eastern and Western Church and, according to a tradition that dates back to an epoch close to that of the Apostles, for priests in general in the Latin Church, can only be understood and lived if is based on this basic structure.

The sublime worth of priestly celibacy makes the acts of sexual abuse committed by some priests particularly abhorrent. Italian journalist Vittorio Messori correctly observed, "If anyone indignantly denounces those vile acts, it is because he gauges the loftiness of the message that [the ministers of God] proclaim to the world, which he would rather not see bespattered, whether or not he is a believer." [2]

---

[2] Vittorio Messori, "Only the Vatican Seems to Make the News", *Corriere della Sera*, March 11, 2010.

Such acts of abuse, which are certainly not limited to ecclesiastical circles and for which celibacy cannot be blamed, manifest instead the spread of a hedonistic culture imbued with eroticism and oblivious to divine judgment. Priestly celibacy is opposed precisely to this trend; not only that: it challenges a culture for which everything is provisional and relative, which tends to deny man's ability to make a lifelong commitment. To such a mindset priestly celibacy appears downright impossible, inhuman, so much so that people are prone to think that anyone who embraces it cannot help practicing it hypocritically.

Today therefore celibacy acquires a particular value as a splendid witness to the fact that "God alone suffices" (Saint Teresa of Avila). "A very meaningful sign", the pope called it in his book-length interview *Light of the World*.[3] The God of the philosophers and the theologians is one thing; more than that, though, our world needs the God of the apostles, of the disciples of Jesus Christ, in whom he continues to make himself present and to act.

Arturo Cattaneo

---

[3] Peter Seewald, *Light of the World: The Pope, the Church and the Signs of the Times* (San Francisco: Ignatius Press, 2010), p. 149.

Priestly Celibacy: A Bit of History

1 Is not priestly celibacy a now outmoded remnant of the ritual purity required of priests in the Old Testament?

It is true that there are elements of continuity between the Old and the New Testaments, but it is also true that Jesus Christ signified, in many aspects, a major innovation. One of these aspects is certainly the value of celibacy. Even though emphasis was placed on continence in the priesthood of the first centuries, the point of reference was the example and the mission of Christ and not the ritual purity of the Old Testament. And so it must be said that the latter was reinterpreted as a prefiguration and image of the salvific action of Christ. In order to grasp the motivation for it, we must recall its main characteristics.

The book of Leviticus (22:4–5) lists some of the criteria of purity that prevent the Old Testament priest from eating the consecrated offerings and, a fortiori, from performing the cultic acts; besides the skin disease that is often but incorrectly translated as "leprosy", diseases of a sexual nature and impurity resulting from contact with a corpse, the prohibition also concerns the "emission of semen". What is meant by this expression is explained by Leviticus 15:16–18: the emission of semen makes a man impure not only in general but also when it occurs during sexual relations; indeed, in this case the impurity involves the woman also, and the duty of purification is likewise extended to her. The condition of sexual purity necessary in order to eat sacred food is required not only of priests: in 1 Samuel 20:26 the absence of David from a sacrificial banquet is attributed to a case of *pollutio nocturna*, whereas in 1 Samuel 21:5 the priest Ahimelech, before allowing David and his companions to eat, by way of exception, the sacred bread, stipulates as the sole condition that they had not had relations with women. Jewish tradition expanded on the biblical precept: the Mishna (T. Babli, *Yoma* 1:1–7) prescribes that the high priest who has prepared to celebrate the rite of the Day of Expiation should be segregated during the preceding night and should be kept awake by youths commissioned for this task, who would tap him by means of wands so as to avoid all contact. This was done precisely out of fear that, if he fell asleep, he could have a nocturnal emission that would render him impure and thus unable to perform the celebration the next day.

The reason why sperm and sexual discharges of, for example, a woman who has given birth (Lev 12:2–5), a woman who is menstruating (Lev 15:19–23) or a person (man or woman) afflicted with gonorrhea (Lev 15:2–12, 25–27) make a person impure is a much-debated topic, but it appears that the reason is to be found in the fact that these things symbolize a loss of life. The God of Israel is the God of life (Deut 5:26; Ps 84:2), the God who gives breath to every living thing (Num 27:16); the dead do not praise him (Ps 115:17), and he is not interested in the dead (Ps 88:10). Whatever recalls death, therefore, is contrary to him and impure, especially a corpse and the "leper", a sort of walking corpse, but also the loss of those fluids on which the transmission of life depends: sperm and menstrual blood. Further evidence of this is contained in the famous verse Leviticus 17:11:

"For the life of the flesh is in the blood; and I have given it for you upon the altar to make atonement for your souls; for it is the blood that makes atonement, by reason of the life." The altar, contaminated by the impurities of the Israelites, is purified by the application of blood—granted by God—and thus once more made worthy to serve as the meeting place between God and his people.

The reason why, in the New Testament, impurity resulting from the discharge of sexual fluid no longer has any reason to exist lies not so much in a more ethical and less ritual character of New Testament religion as rather in the fact that the blood of Christ shed on the Cross, the supremely life-giving element, purifies all impurities once and for all, reestablishing life where hitherto death had reigned (Heb 9:11–14; Rom 3:24–25). Therefore there is no longer a need for the shedding of purifying sacrificial blood, because in Christ everything is pure, so much so that the marital act is no longer marked by death but becomes the image of the union between Christ and the Church (cf. Eph 5:25–27). Even the second great source of impurity, the corpse (cf. Num 19:11–16) is purified: the body, being united to the death and burial of Christ (Col 2:12), is sown in corruption and rises in incorruption (cf. 1 Cor 15:42).

From the preceding discussion it is quite clear that the celibacy of priests in the New Testament cannot be thought of as a continuation of the continence of the Old Testament priesthood, but rather as a particular charism of conformity to Christ, the virginal spouse of the Church (cf. Eph 5:31–32), in whose person they act. This is understood along the lines of a renunciation of earthly fruitfulness so as to affirm a fruitfulness rooted in the definitive union between the ecclesial Bride and her divine Bridegroom, in which she is purified by his blood:

"Not all men can receive this precept, but only those to whom it is given. For there are eunuchs who have been so from birth, and there are eunuchs who have been made eunuchs by men, and there are eunuchs who have made themselves eunuchs for the sake of the kingdom of heaven" (Mt 19:11–12). In the Church's tradition (cf. Innocent I, Epist. 2, 9, 12 *ad Victricium*: PL 20:475C–477A), in continuity with the ascetical teaching of Paul that sexual abstinence fosters prayer (cf. 1 Cor 7:5), Old Testament cultic continence was then reinterpreted in terms of priestly celibacy, as a practical guideline for living out a conformity to Christ that had another basis altogether. "Merely functional" interpretations of celibacy, and subsequent requests for the abolition or mitigation thereof, thus prove to be out of place (cf. Benedict XVI, *Sacramentum Caritatis*, no. 24).

Giorgio Paximadi

2 Is priestly celibacy a discipline of the Latin Church, or does it have biblical origins?

1. The meaning of Jesus' celibacy

The Gospels agree in testifying that Jesus of Nazareth maintained what no one had ever before dared to say: that the God of Israel, his Father, had sent him to reveal definitively his own unconditionally loving face and to *offer eternal life to all who believed in him* (Mt 19:29 and parallels; Jn 3:15–16, 36; 4:14, etc.). By word and deed, Jesus announced that the kingdom of God had drawn near through him (cf. Mt 4:17; 10:7 and parallels; Lk 10:11; 21:31) and thus had been made present in the world (cf. Mt 12:28 and parallels; Lk 17:21).

In order to testify that, as the Son, he had received from God the Father the divine life in which he wanted all men to share (cf. Jn 5:26; Mt 11:27), Jesus worked many extraordinary "signs", which often were miracles of mercy. And so, like the prophets Isaiah (8:18) and Ezekiel (12:11; 24:24), *he himself became a sign of revelation* (cf. Mt 12:38–40; 16:4 and parallels; Mt 24:30). In particular, like the prophets Jeremiah (16:2) and John the Baptist, he too lived as a celibate, without marrying and having children.

From this perspective too, Christ appeared as a "sign of contradiction" (Lk 2:34) with respect to Judaism; for the great majority of Jews, celibacy was a humiliating condition (cf. Judg 11:37). And yet Christ deliberately made this choice (cf. Mt 19:11–12), declaring—perhaps to defend himself from certain rumors that were circulating about him and the Twelve—that he had made himself a "eunuch" permanently "for the sake of the kingdom of heaven" (Mt 19:12). For what purpose? No doubt, so as to dedicate all his energies to the proclamation of the kingdom of God, free—both practically and emotionally—from any family ties (cf. Lk 9:58–62 and parallels). But above all, because of the intrinsic connection between that choice and the very content of his proclamation. *Jesus Christ did not marry and did not have children so as to communicate in a "fleshly" way as well*—since he had become "flesh" precisely for this purpose (cf. Jn 1:14, 18)—*that the eternal life he was offering to every human being came originally and exclusively from God the Father.*

Moreover, in Jesus' time, the Hebrews learned from the Old Testament tradition that God the Creator is the wellspring of eternal life, in other words, the source of a covenant relationship with him that is capable of going beyond death (cf. 2 Mac 7:9, 23, 36; Wis 1:13–14; 2:23; 6:19). But they were waiting for the definitive mediator with God—the Messiah—who was supposed to inaugurate the "new covenant" (Jer 31:31–34) by purifying them of sin with the divine Spirit (cf. Ezek 11:19–20; 36:25–29) and giving them eternal life (cf. Is 25:6–10a).

Within the context of the multiform messianic hopes of the era, Jesus showed that he had an altogether unique filial relationship with God, his Father, yet he wanted to bring his disciples into it also. Therefore he taught them: "Call no man your father on earth, for you have one Father, who is in heaven" (Mt 23:9). This teaching expressed not only the surpassing of family ties to affirm

the absolute primacy of God; in the first place it specified that God is the one Father of all, the origin of all
fatherhood (cf. Eph 3:14–15), *in other words, the unique
source* of both the physical life and the eternal life of every
human being. It is no accident, then, that Jesus did not
have others call him "father", thus distancing himself from
the custom of calling prophets (cf. 2 Kings 2:12; 6:21;
13:14), wise men (cf. 2 Mac 14:37), teachers (cf. Acts
23:6) and priests (cf. Judg 17:10; 18:19) by that title.

Convinced that the Lord was the sole Father of all and
that all were children of God and brethren to one another
(cf. Mt 23:8), Christ insisted repeatedly that his disciples
should behave as "brethren" (cf. Mt. 5:22–24, 47; 7:3–5;
18:15, 21, 35, etc.). He himself called them "his brethren"
(Mt 28:10; Jn 20:17–18; cf. Mt 25:40).

And so Jesus went so far as to subordinate familial ties
(cf. Mt 12:46–50 and parallels; Lk 8:19–21; 11:28) to
his fraternal relationship with the disciples (cf. Mt 10:37
and parallels), declaring: "Whoever does the will of my
Father in heaven is my brother, and sister, and mother"
(Mt 12:49–50). Hence the fraternal ties that Jesus created among his disciples and, in particular, among the
Twelve (cf. Mk 3:13–14 and parallels) were based, through
him, on the unconditionally kind fatherhood of his Father,
which then constituted the very nucleus of the good news
that he proclaimed and incarnated.

Therefore, *in order to bear witness*, without any possibility of ambiguity, *that God the Father alone was to generate children to the eternal life* that he possessed and gave
(Jn 5:26), Jesus not only allowed no one to call him
"father" but also lived in celibacy and in perfect continence, without marrying and having children.

More precisely, the Son, through his evangelizing activity, certainly allowed his Father to generate children for

eternal life. Jesus did not marry, however, nor did he pro-
create children, in order to reveal the non-bodily way in
which God generates, through his Son and through his
Spirit (cf. Rom 8:15; Gal 4:6).

Emblematically, Jesus, unlike the rabbis of his day,
allowed women to become his followers (cf. Mt 27:55
and parallels; Mt 27:61 and parallels; Lk 8:2–3) and to
listen to his words (cf. Lk 10:39, 42). And so he experienced also a genuine, mature friendship with several
women (cf. Lk 10:38–42; Jn 11:5; 12:2–3) and declared
that their faith in him was salvific (cf. Mt 9:22 and parallels). But precisely by means of his celibacy and perfect
continence, Christ showed that it is only through a faith-
filled affection for him that any woman—without discrimination based on her sex (cf. Gal 3:28)—can consider
herself his "sister" (Mt 12:50 and parallels), being a daugh-
ter of the one Father.

To summarize, we can say that Jesus *did not generate
children physically*, but loved his disciples as "brethren" and
shared a common life with the Twelve, yet without ever
allowing anyone to call him "father"; thereby he offered
several clear "signs" of the unique fatherhood of God
and of his own identity as the only-begotten Son of the
Father (cf. Jn 1:14, 18; 3:16, 18, etc.), with a mandate
from God to lead his children to divine glory (cf. Heb
2:10). To this end, the Son, having received divine life
from the Father, made sharers in it those who believed
in him (cf. Mt 19:28–29 and parallels; Jn 3:15–16, 36,
etc.) and, in particular, the Twelve.

In the second place, *by generating children "spiritually"*,
but remaining celibate and continent, Jesus gave his disciples to understand that the divine communication of
eternal life occurs "not of perishable seed" (1 Pet 1:23)
nor "of blood nor of the will of the flesh nor of the will

of man" (Jn 1:13). Therefore Jesus' way of communicating divine life is not the way of physical generation (cf. Mt 3:9 and parallels), but the way of spiritual (re)generation (cf. Mt 3:11 and parallels; 1 Pet 1:3), "from above", "by the Spirit" of God (Jn 3:3, 5–8).

It follows from both the preceding remarks that Jesus' choice to be celibate and permanently continent "for the sake of the kingdom of heaven" (Mt 19:12) was a "sign" capable of manifesting this truth of faith: God the Father is the sole source of eternal life, which Jesus, as the only-begotten Son, received as a gift and which he, as the definitive saving mediator (cf. 1 Tim 2:5; Heb 8:6; 9:15; 12:24), communicated to his disciples. But this truth of faith is precisely the gospel of Christ. Therefore the *form* of Jesus' earthly life, which was intentionally celibate, continent and fraternal, expresses the very *content* of his proclamation concerning the definitive coming of the kingdom of God into the world: anyone who believes in Jesus and lives as he does becomes a child of God "in" him (cf. Jn 1:12; Rom 8:29; Gal 3:26–27); in other words, he receives the gift of divine life that comes from the Father and is offered unconditionally to every human being by the same Christ, who has risen through his Spirit.

2. The meaning of the celibacy of the Twelve

In imitation of Jesus, the Twelve lived together as brothers, because he, the only-begotten Son of the Father, made them so (cf. Jn 1:12; Rom 8:29). Loving them "to the end" (Jn 13:1), in other words, even to his death on the Cross for them (cf. Jn 19:30), Jesus demonstrated to them how utterly and unconditionally God loved them and wished them to love one another as brothers in the same way (cf. Mt 5:44–48; Lk 6:27, 32–33, 36), that is, "as" Jesus had loved them (Jn 13:34; 15:12).

Therefore there is an extremely important connection between Jesus' experience of brotherhood with the Twelve and his choice to live in permanent celibacy and continence: it was precisely by living fraternally with the Twelve that he gave *to them primarily* a share in the eternal life of the Father. But this gift of his was none other than the "good news"—the "gospel"—manifested by him *to all* as well through the "sign" of celibacy and perfect continence.

Consequently *the choice of the Twelve* to "leave everything"—even their families—(cf. Mt 19:27 and parallels) so as to live with Jesus in a way that was fraternal and celibate—or at least continent, in the case of those like Peter, who had already been married (cf. Mt 8:14–15 and parallels)—*had one sole purpose: to witness "as" he was doing* (Jn 13:34; 15:12) *to the "good news" of God-Abba* (Mk 14:36; cf. Rom 8:15; Gal 4:6); that is, to announce that God is an unconditionally good Father who "spiritually" generates to eternal life all who believe in the Son, although previously they had been scattered in the blind alleys of sin (Jn 11:52).

3. The meaning of ministerial celibacy in the apostolic Church

The celibate, continent and fraternal *form* of Jesus' life with the Twelve was taken, even in the apostolic age, as a particularly eloquent "sign" of his very "gospel". Indeed, while living "in remembrance of" Christ (cf. Lk 22:19; 1 Cor 11:25), the New Testament authors bore witness in writing to the fruitful ecclesial consequences of their awareness in faith that eternal life, coming from God the

Father, is offered universally by the Spirit of the Risen Lord. Thus they resorted to the maternal metaphor for the Church as such and to the paternal metaphor for the apostolic ministry.

The maternal metaphor (cf. for example Jn 19:26–27; Gal 4:19, 22–31; 1 Thess 2:7–8; 2 Jn 1; Rev 12) expresses the shared responsibility of the members of the Church— and, above all, of her ordained ministers—to make sure that all people have the opportunity to become children of God, brethren of Christ and brethren to one another.

The paternal metaphor, on the other hand, is used especially by Saint Paul to indicate his own educational role (cf. 1 Thess 2:10–12; Philem 10) or else to claim, as opposed to other missionaries, his own "primacy" in evangelizing a particular Christian community (cf. 1 Cor 4:14–15). In the latter case too, however, the apostle's job of generating faith-filled members of that community is carried out though his participation in the unique and definitive saving mediation of Christ.

In any case, there is still in the New Testament authors a clear awareness that divine life is generated in Christians by God the Father, through the definitive saving mediation of his Son Jesus, by the power of the Holy Spirit (cf. 1 Jn 5:11–12 etc.).

The meaning of the celibacy of apostles such as Paul must be understood *within this perspective of the "spiritual" transmission of eternal life*, which has in God its paternal source and in the Church, enlivened by the Spirit of the Risen Lord, its maternal mediation. Indeed, Paul carried out his own ministry as a celibate (cf. 1 Cor 7:7, 9:5; Phil 3:7–8) and in *teamwork* with other missionaries (cf. Acts 15:22; Rom 16:3, 9, 21; 2 Cor 8:23; Phil 4:3; 1 Thess 3:2). Inscribing the forms of evangelical charity (cf. 1 Cor 13) in the various emotional registers of his rich personality, the apostle became "all things to all men" (1 Cor 9:22) in his evangelizing mission, inspired as he was by the same "mind ... which was in Christ Jesus" (Phil 2:5; cf. 2 Cor 4:10–12; 13:4).

Therefore, Paul understood himself to be the friend of Christ, who in a spousal way "loved the Church and gave himself up for her" (Eph 5:25). As "the friend of the bridegroom", for example, the apostle went so far as to declare that he experienced a sort of divine "jealousy" (cf. Ezek 16:42) of the Christian community in Corinth. He himself had evangelized it, thus "betrothing it" to Christ (2 Cor 11:2). Hence Paul's serious preoccupation with that community, which was in danger of betraying Jesus (cf. 2 Cor 11:4), abandoning him for heresy. But, beyond that particular case, we can understand how the apostle identified himself to such an extent with Christ (cf. Gal 2:20; 2 Cor 4:10; Phil 1:21) that he imitated him (cf. 1 Cor 11:1; 1 Thess 1:6), to the point of deciding to love the Church with his whole strength (cf. Eph 5:31–32, which cites Gen 2:24) and to testify, in his ecclesial dedication, to the Father's loving offer of life, by means of a celibate, continent and fraternal management of his own emotional capacities.

The ultimate purpose of Paul's apostolic mission, experienced *in this way* with his "brothers" in ministry (cf. 1 Cor 1:1; 16:12; 2 Cor 1:1; 2:13; 8:22; Eph 6:21 etc.), was to form "Christ" in Christians and to make him grow in them (Gal 4:19); in other words, to generate a divine life conformed to that of Christ (cf. Rom 8:29; Phil 3:10, 21). This is how we must understand his admission that he continues to "be in travail" with Christians (Gal 4:19): obviously it was a question of generating them "spiritually", that is, by the power of the life-giving Spirit of the Risen Lord (cf. Gal 5:25; Jn 6:63; Rom 8:11; 1 Cor 15:45;

2 Cor 3:6; 1 Pet 3:18), first through baptism and then by means of pastoral care that was not without suffering.

Given this concept of the apostolic Church, how can we understand, finally, the rule in the pastoral letters of Paul that says candidates for the episcopacy (1 Tim 3:2), the presbyterate (Tit 1:6) and the diaconate (1 Tim 3:12) should be "the husband of one wife"? This stereotypical formula, which is never used in the letters written for other Christians, has been understood by some contemporary scholars above all in the light of the interpretation given to it by Pope Saint Siricius (384–99) and that seen in the many testimonies to the obligation of continence for bishops, priests and deacons that was already in force in various Eastern and Western regions of the Church. From the decretals *Directa* (385) and *Cum in unum* (386), it is apparent that having been married only once would attest the ability of a candidate to major orders—whether married or widowed—to live in perfect continence after ordination. It turns out, therefore, that from the time of the composition of the First Letter of Paul to Timothy and the Letter of Paul to Titus, bishops, priests and deacons were expected to practice complete continence.

A regulation of this sort, for married clerics also—who *thus renounced physical generation*—could be based on the testimony of the Gospels, inasmuch as it allowed bishops, priests and deacons to "commemorate"—indeed, to "be a remembrance" of—Christ, who, through a celibate, continent and fraternal life with the Twelve, testified to God-Abba, enabling him to *generate "spiritually"* children for eternal life.

In summary, according to the New Testament witness, the *fraternal, continent or absolutely celibate way of life* practiced by the Twelve and by various evangelizers of the apostolic Church, who by their lives imitated Christ, is a highly important "sign" for witnessing to the *central content* of the "gospel" itself. This can be identified as the fundamental biblical reason why celibacy continues to be in force for the bishops of the whole Church—bishops in both the East and the West—and for priests in the Latin Church.

Franco Manzi

3   Is it true that priestly celibacy did not develop until the Middle Ages?

Priestly celibacy is one of the oldest ecclesiastical traditions. Christ did not marry and had no children. That is the great example that the apostles emulated. Even those who were already married left their wives and children so as to follow Christ (cf. Mk 10:28–30). Of course, that does not mean they deserted their wives: their wives did not remain behind alone but took shelter in the extended family. The apostles themselves, however, wanted to follow Christ radically, and that was possible only without family obligations. In early Christianity, abstinence (which is also called continence) played a much more important role than is generally admitted. Research will certainly bring still more to light to this topic in the next few years on the basis of new questions that have been posed. The radical lifestyle of Christ's disciples, which also included the permanent renunciation of sex, continued to have influence over the centuries. Admittedly, well into the High Middle Ages married men were allowed to be ordained and to remain married; after their ordination, however, they had to practice continence, while their single or widowed confreres could no longer marry after priestly ordination.

Concerning the historical origin of celibacy it is therefore important to recognize that, until the High Middle Ages, the concept of celibacy was more extensive than it is today. It was not just about forbidding marriage for single priests, but also about a "celibacy of continence": all deacons, priests and bishops, whether they were now married, widowed or single, had to refrain from all sexual activity from the day of their ordination and were not allowed to beget children. Consequently, it was not just about an occasional cultic chastity—for instance, on the day before celebrating the Eucharist—but rather about permanent continence for the purpose of being able to serve the Church unreservedly. The concept of celibacy was therefore more comprehensive than it is today: whereas celibacy today applies only to single priests, in the early Church it applied also to married priests, who had to live as though in a Josephite marriage and renounce sexual relations. Nowhere in the early Church can it be proved that a married cleric legitimately begat children after his ordination.

Today, of course, there are misgivings about such a practice: How could the Church demand of legitimately married Christians that they should suddenly live in complete continence? And is permanent continence within marriage even thinkable? We must, however, keep in mind the societal context at the time. Clerical office was considered prestigious, and hence it was quite appropriate to make sacrifices for it. The wife of a cleric, furthermore, had to consent explicitly to the ordination of her husband. Clerics were ordained at an age that in those days was already advanced (*viri probati*), when their own children were already grown or even had left the household and family life could be subordinated to the demands of an ecclesiastical vocation. And, finally, we must not forget that medicine in those days recommended, for reasons of health and hygiene, engaging in sexual relations exclusively for procreative purposes. Nevertheless, continence for married clerics remained problematic with respect to the sacramentality of marriage. During the course of the Middle Ages, this led ultimately to the insight that it was better to do without married clerics than to require continence of them and their wives. And so developed the current practice, which after the Council of Trent (1545–63) became definitive and generally accepted, namely, that of ordaining to the priesthood only candidates who were still unmarried—a considerable mitigation of the continence discipline.

It is scarcely possible to mention here all the patristic testimonies, starting with Clement of Alexandria and Tertullian of Carthage down to John Chrysostom and Jerome, as well as the numerous conciliar decisions that dealt with clerical continence and celibacy in the early Church. From around 200, references to the practice of clerical continence become more common in East and West. Certainly no comprehensive picture emerges from them; the literary sources are too sparse. Yet it can be said with historical certainty that the continence of married deacons, priests and bishops more and more clearly becomes an obligation, precisely because of the example of Jesus himself and of the apostles. Thus, from the third century on, the general trend is unambiguously in the direction of an unmarried clergy. In any case, the fact that some clerics are married is, within the Church, no argument against continence or against celibacy. On the contrary, the faithful expect continence even from their married clergymen, and they prefer an unmarried clergy. The first norm recorded in writing that requires continence for married ministers in the West is canon 33 of the Council of Elvira, which took place around the year 308. This does not mean, however, that the practice codified in Elvira had not already been customary before then.

The Christian monastic movement is often cited as evidence that clerical continence and celibacy actually arose only with the beginning of monasticism in the fourth century. In this connection, people like to maintain that the ascetical movement started by monasticism and its antipathy toward the body is fundamentally foreign to the priesthood. Consequently, the argument goes, we must distinguish the celibacy of monks from the living situation of priests who were married and having children. In my opinion, precisely the opposite is true: in the beginning there was the continence of Jesus, the apostles and the clergy (deacons, priests, bishops) until rather late, namely, the fourth century, when the monastic movement started in Egypt and drew terrific crowds. But clerical continence had already become widespread centuries earlier. Many texts from the second through the fourth centuries, from both the West and the East, could be cited that tend to show a connection between the priesthood and perfect continence.

The boom in monasticism seems, however, to have had at least one consequence in the fourth century: the Church investigated more carefully the theological justification for clerical continence. For those clerics living in the world, an ascetical basis for continence would not do—asceticism was the monks' business; rather, a sacramental basis had to be found. Accordingly the argument for priestly continence was based not on a preference for a stricter lifestyle but rather on the office of the deacon, the priest and the bishop himself. Clerics must practice continence because they are ministers of the sacraments and must dedicate themselves entirely to this service.

According to the teaching of Popes Siricius and Innocent, clerical continence is indispensable. It is founded on the acts of Christ himself, who wrought our salvation as an unmarried man. Jesus had no other life to hand on than the one that he laid down on the Cross. In him we are saved, redeemed, reborn—not by procreation, not by the will of the flesh, but in his blood. This gift of himself is accomplished again and again in the chalice of the Eucharist and through those who *in persona Christi* repeat the words: "Take and eat, take and drink, this is my Body, this is my Blood." One suspects that the celibacy of Christ's ministers has a meaning that extends far beyond the purely disciplinary sphere.

Stefan Heid

4 Why do the Eastern and the Western churches differ in the matter of priestly celibacy?

In the first few centuries, the Church in the East was acquainted with clerical continence as was that in the West. It applied to married, never-married and widowed clergy. Today that is quickly forgotten when people speak about the Eastern churches. Interestingly enough, the evidence for clerical continence in the first few centuries is even clearer in the East than in the West. Only since the fifth century did the common discipline crumble. This process of erosion began in the East with the separation of large sectors of the non-Hellenic ecclesiastical provinces from the imperial Church and then continued within the imperial Byzantine Church itself. Today practically all the Eastern churches tend to reject a strict discipline of continence, not to mention Western celibacy. Consequently, in the Eastern churches today, there are married deacons and priests, who have children even after ordination. Despite this, even Eastern clerical discipline still has elements of celibacy, but these lack uniformity. We are talking about remnants of the continence discipline of the early Church; for example, the disqualification of twice-married men, the prohibition against marriage after ordination and, above all, the rule that only unmarried candidates may be admitted to the office of bishop.

The first tremors that weakened the unrestricted duty to practice continence came no doubt from the major schisms that the Church in the East experienced. Thus, for example, the splitting off of the East Syrian, West Syrian and Coptic Christians starting in the fifth century led with varying rapidity to the abandonment of continence. This process is quite clearly evident in the case of the Persian Church, where, after the Council of Ephesus (431), there was a deliberate departure from the practice of continence that had been customary before, because the Persians intended to dissolve their union with the imperial Byzantine Church and to have nothing more to do with it politically. This resulted in a separate Church of Persia, which made itself autonomous in its organization and discipline.

Egypt faced a special situation inasmuch as it was the birthplace of monasticism. The Coptic (i.e., Egyptian) Church rightly felt that it was the proud inheritor of this extraordinary success story of Christianity, which looked to the Desert Father Anthony as its most famous ancestor. Given the great esteem in which asceticism was held in this church, it is not at all surprising that impressive testimonies can prove the existence there of clerical continence well into the fifth century. Later, however, monasticism became dominant to such an extent that it actually assumed responsibility for the spirituality and pastoral care of the people, and that has basically remained true to this day. The Coptic clergy is mostly monastic and has practically no secular priests.

The imperial Byzantine Church upheld the ideal of a continent clergy for a long time, at least as a formality. In the sixth-century Body of Civil Law of the Emperor Justinian, the prohibition against marriage for clerics is clear; furthermore, men who were already married for the second time could not be ordained. Continence is described as the origin and foundation of the divine canons and of all other virtues. This state of affairs continued until the year 691 at the Council in Trullo (so called after the place where it convened, the emperor's palace in Constantinople), when the Byzantine Church publicly opposed the Latin West, from which it wanted to distinguish itself. For this purpose it cited—whether deliberately or inadvertently is a matter of debate—manipulated (or poorly translated) documents of the North African councils of 390 and 401. These councils had actually declared themselves in favor of strict and comprehensive clerical continence, but they were twisted by the Council in Trullo to mean the exact opposite.

Recent historical research has been able to prove unmistakably the development from a unified practice throughout the Church to a relaxation of clerical continence in the Eastern churches. This view, however, is not yet universally accepted—especially not by those who still cling uncritically to the misleading yet widespread opinion (in the West at least) that celibacy did not exist until the Middle Ages and that it was an invention of the Latin Church.

The response to this is that it would be helpful if Eastern church historiography could include two indisputable findings of scholarly research in its considerations. The first point was already mentioned: the Council in Trullo is based on manipulated North African council documents that do not accurately reflect the Latin tradition. The second point concerns the notorious Paphnutius legend, which still makes its spectral appearance in many Eastern rebuttals of celibacy. According to this legend, the First Council of Nicaea in the year 325 unanimously rejected clerical continence, declaring that it was impossible to require continence of married couples. Scholarly studies fifty years ago, however, proved that the document declaring this rejection is a forgery. Nevertheless, since the document had already made its way into a Byzantine history book that met with general acclaim in the East, it has the status of being an established fact and remains influential to this day.

The Eastern interpretation must therefore be rejected, because in historical terms it is untenable. The best Greek Fathers of the Church in the first centuries propagated clerical continence, and the highly esteemed Epiphanius of Salamis, to mention only the most prominent and widely recognized example, speaks unmistakably about indispensable clerical continence, whereby he means exactly the same discipline that prevailed at that time in the Latin West. Ecumenical dialogue today can start with these historical insights and perhaps arrive at a new consensus.

Stefan Heid

5 The churches in the East have allowed the priestly ordination of married men. Could not the Latin Church do the same?

This would go against the most ancient tradition, recognized by Eastern Christians also, that required perfect continence of priests. Indeed, there are good reasons to maintain that the common practice in the East and the West, before the Council in Trullo, was to draw clergy, for the most part, from the ranks of married candidates of an advanced age (*presbyters* means "elders"), provided, however, that they, with the consent of their wives, would pledge to live thereafter in total and perpetual continence. In recent decades a growing number of experts in historical research maintain that the practice of the Church in the early centuries did allow married priests, but on the condition that after ordination they would live in perfect and perpetual continence (C. Cochini, R. Cholij, A. M. Stickler, S. Heid, L. Touze).

The requirement for perfect continence reflects the intuition—at that time not yet formulated theologically, yet perceived by the ecclesial consciousness—that there is a congruence between celibacy and priesthood. Indeed, many Christians probably sensed from the beginning that the priest should be free from any other all-encompassing tie, so as to be able to give himself to the Church in a fully spousal way, after the example of Christ himself. Therefore, as a first step, perfect continence was required of married candidates and cohabitation with a wife was absolutely prohibited. For example, the First Council of Nicaea (325) decreed: "The great Council has absolutely forbidden bishops, priests, and deacons—in other words, all the members of the clergy—to have with them a sister-companion with the exception of a mother, a sister, an aunt, or, lastly, only those persons who are beyond any suspicion." Soon, however, many realized that prohibiting marital unity contradicted the very nature of the sacrament of matrimony and that it was not reasonable to require separation from a legitimate spouse.

Considering the unseemliness of prohibiting conjugal relations between legitimately married spouses, the logical development was that the Latin Church tended more and more to seek celibate candidates (from the ninth century on, celibate candidates were ordained almost exclusively), thus safeguarding the spousal meaning of the priesthood. In the East, on the other hand, starting with the Byzantine Council in Trullo (691), marital relations were permitted for married clergy when they were not performing their service at the altar, thus making less evident the all-encompassing character of the spousal dimension of the priesthood. Consequently, daily celebration of the Eucharist by married priests declined in the East (because otherwise they would need to abstain constantly from marital relations).

A further reflection can be made in support of the discipline of the Latin Church. Today there is no longer any doubt about the fact that the episcopate constitutes the fullness of the sacrament of holy orders. This has led theology to explain the presbyterate in terms of the episcopate. Thus theologians have become increasingly aware that not only the bishops but also the priests make present Christ, the Head and Bridegroom of the Church. Consequently it is understandable why the discipline that in the East as well as in the West always required celibacy-continence for the episcopate, should logically apply—at least to a large extent—to the presbyterate also.

It can be stated therefore that the Latin Church, with its progressive introduction, from the fourth century on, of the celibacy requirement for young aspirants to the priesthood (in other words, by selecting only unmarried candidates), has remained in tune with the original practice of a perfectly continent clergy.

The "mitigated" discipline introduced by the Council in Trullo is in force in most of the Eastern churches and has been accepted by the Church of Rome, though the Holy See has established certain restrictions for the married Eastern-rite priests who carry out their ministry in the West.

If, with regard to priestly celibacy, one wanted to foster a uniform discipline between the Latin Church and the Eastern churches, it would be logical to promote the celibate priesthood in the Eastern churches too, while still respecting their proper disciplinary autonomy. Indeed, Vatican II, in recommending celibacy, declared that it did not mean to impose a change in the current discipline in the Eastern churches (cf. *Presbyterorum Ordinis*, no. 16a). Just recently the Syro-Malankar Church and the Syro-Malabar Church independently confirmed the celibacy requirement for their priests.

Pablo Gefaell

6 Is it true that with the personal ordinariates for the Anglican faithful there is now an opening for married priests?

The very institution of personal ordinariates for Anglicans who enter into full communion with the Catholic Church has demonstrated that the pope considers it important to uphold the celibacy requirement even for them.

Indeed, another possible plan would have been to create a new ritual church and to confer on it the faculty of ordaining married men, as has been the case for most of the Eastern-rite churches that are in full communion with the Catholic Church.

With the apostolic constitution *Anglicanorum Coetibus* (November 4, 2009), the pope instead instituted personal ordinariates to welcome the Anglican faithful who want to enter into full communion with the Catholic Church, stressing in that constitution the need to observe existing norms with regard to celibacy (cf. VI § 1). The fact that married Anglican priests who enter the Catholic Church can receive priestly ordination in it is nothing new. Indeed, for several decades the Church has frequently dispensed from the celibacy requirement, so that married Anglican clergy who want to continue their ministerial service as Catholic priests can be ordained in the Catholic Church.

A certain innovation regarding celibacy can be discerned in the following paragraph from the constitution: "The Ordinary, in full observance of the discipline of celibate clergy in the Latin Church, as a rule (*pro regula*) will admit only celibate men to the order of presbyter. He may also petition the Roman Pontiff, as a derogation from can. 277, §1, for the admission of married men to the order of presbyter on a case by case basis, according to objective criteria approved by the Holy See" (VI § 2). This "opening", however, having been prudently formulated, is transitory; in fact, it is plainly intended to accommodate those Anglicans clergy who are already married and preparing to receive holy orders in the Roman Catholic Church.

Arturo Cattaneo

7 Would not permission to ordain married men foster an increase in vocations?

One of the most frequently recurring arguments for abandoning obligatory celibacy is the need to increase vocations to the priesthood, above all in countries where there is a major priest shortage. Hence in recent decades there have been repeated proposals to ordain *viri probati*, in other words, married laymen of a certain age and proven faith.

In this regard it must be said immediately that there is in fact no evidence that requiring less of candidates to the priesthood leads to increased numbers of them. Experience proves the contrary instead: vocations to the priesthood flourish and multiply precisely when the radical gospel message is welcomed consistently and unapologetically. One may recall too that a shortage of vocations has occurred also in other Christian denominations—such as the Anglicans and the Lutherans—that do not have obligatory celibacy.

To increase vocations to the priesthood it is necessary, rather, to recognize the principle reason for the lack of them: the weakening of the faith, which leads to greater difficulty in perceiving the closeness of Christ, who loves us, calls us and asks us to follow him. It should be noted, moreover, that for many people it has become hard to appreciate the Church as a gift of God and a mission in which to become involved. In the West, another factor not to be underestimated is the deliberate limitation of family size, which then leads parents to dissuade their sons from aspiring to the priesthood.

To promote vocations to the priesthood, Cardinal Mauro Piacenza remarked, it is therefore "necessary, in an ever more deafening world, to create new spaces of silence and listening by providing spiritual direction and sacramental confession for young men, so that God's voice, which still continues to call, may be heard and followed promptly".[1] The Lord himself has shown us the way to obtain more vocations: "Pray therefore the Lord of the harvest to send out laborers into his harvest" (Mt 9:38). The truly efficacious weapon in any campaign to increase vocations is therefore prayer.

As for the number of vocations, it is inappropriate, however, to compare the Church to a business that cannot function without a certain number of personnel in management. "Our Lord Jesus Christ did not hesitate to confide the formidable task of evangelizing the world, as it was then known, to a handful of men to all appearances lacking in number and quality. He bade this 'little flock' not to lose heart, for, thanks to his constant assistance, through him and with him, they would overcome the world" (*Sacerdotalis Caelibatus, no.* 47).

Arturo Cattaneo

---

[1] *L'Osservatore Romano*, Italian edition, June 19, 2009.

What Theology Says on the Subject

8 Is it true that Vatican II describes priestly celibacy not as necessary but merely as "appropriate"?

The Second Vatican Council indeed describes celibacy not as necessary but as appropriate. According to the *Decree on the Ministry and Life of Priests*, celibacy "is not demanded of the priesthood by its nature. This is clear from the practice of the primitive Church and the tradition of the Eastern Churches where in addition to those—including all bishops—who choose from the gift of grace to preserve celibacy, there are also many excellent married priests.... There are many ways in which celibacy is in harmony with the priesthood" (*Presbyterorum Ordinis*, no. 16). This has led some to maintain that priestly celibacy is appropriate in certain historical circumstances but may be inappropriate in others; for example, in the current situation.

In this regard it must be pointed out that the concept of "appropriateness" or "convenience" in theology implies the "convergence" or agreement of various considerable reasons, even though they may not amount to a "necessity", strictly speaking.

According to the above-mentioned conciliar decree, there is no connection of strict necessity between the ministerial priesthood and celibacy. As evidence for this, the decree mentions the practices of the primitive Church and those of the churches in the East. It should be noted here that the council could not yet take into account the findings of historical research in recent decades, which show that disciplinary regulations about clerical continence do date from the fourth century yet presupposed an older tradition, which can be traced directly back to the example of Christ and to the ordinances of the apostles.

On a purely theoretical plane, a necessary connection between ministerial priesthood and celibacy could proceed from two reasons: either an intrinsic requirement (if the fact of priesthood simply ruled out the possibility of marriage) or an ordinance of Christ himself, which would oblige even without logically compelling reasons (this is true, for example, of the practice of using only bread and wine and not other beverages and foods for the Eucharist: symbolic and biblical reasons can be adduced for the choice of bread and wine, but the decisive argument is the will of Christ, who instituted the Eucharist).

In the case of celibacy, however, there can be no question of an intrinsic necessity, because marriage is not an evil but rather a reality that comes from God, the Creator, and was raised by Christ to the status of a sacrament for baptized spouses. An ordinance of Christ, in contrast, could concern the apostles and, thus, all their successors who hold the same position—that is, the bishops, who have received the fullness of the sacrament of holy orders. For this reason some theologians think that the Church will never be able to abolish the continence requirement for bishops. This discussion among theologians has not yet been decided. Interestingly enough, the statement that celibacy does not follow necessarily from the nature of the priesthood appears in the conciliar decree on priests, but not in the conciliar decree on bishops.

In conclusion, it should be emphasized that priestly celibacy, which in "many ways ... is in harmony with

the priesthood", is not only based on a disciplinary regulation in this regard, but also looks to the recommen-
dation of Jesus Christ himself, which is based on the
example of his own life (the council cites Mt 19:12).
Furthermore, reference should be made to the advan-
tages of Christian celibacy, as Paul explains them (cf. 1
Cor 7:25–40), as well as the profound agreement between
the reasons for celibacy and the theological profile of the
priestly ministry. The clearest magisterial discussion of
this topic can be found in the encyclical by Paul VI on
priestly celibacy (1967).

Manfred Hauke

9 Celibacy is not a dogma but only a disciplinary norm. Why does the Church still attach such great importance to it?

It is true that priestly celibacy is not dogmatically necessary—but this does not mean that it is a merely disciplinary measure. The various arguments for priestly celibacy have condensed over the course of the centuries into one central requirement: namely, that the priest should be similar to Christ, the Good Shepherd and Bridegroom of the Church. Magisterial documents and theologians have both emphasized this again and again in recent decades.

Essentially the priestly vocation consists of following the example of Christ and living as he did. This has to do not merely with the fact that Christ was unmarried, but rather with the deeper reason for this celibacy: Jesus regarded himself as the "Bridegroom" of the whole community of believers—a community that, as is already anticipated in Old Testament imagery, becomes his "Bride". The Old Testament prophets already described the covenant between God and his people as a "marriage", in which the "Bridegroom" gives himself up for his "Bride", Israel (cf. Mk 2:19–20). That is why Paul's letter to the Ephesians (5:21–33) also uses the image of marriage for the union between Christ and the Church: Christ the

"Bridegroom" gave himself up for his "Bride", so as to make her completely beautiful. Christ's "wedding" with the Church has already begun, but it will be perfected only in the new world, at the end of the ages, when the Lord comes again (cf., for example, Mt 25:1–13; Rev 19:7–8). Then every yearning for happiness will be fulfilled. Logically the wedding feast in Sacred Scripture is also a symbol for the joys of paradise. The celibacy of Jesus Christ expresses his unconditional devotion to and love for all mankind, which is called to become part of the Church in an indissoluble covenant.

Jesus Christ shows the utmost esteem for marriage and perfects it; he himself lives out the mystery to which marriage is ordered in God's plan for salvation: the covenant of love between God and redeemed humanity. That is why he recommends to his disciples a celibate life for the sake of the kingdom of heaven (cf. Mt 19:12). This gift from God, a "charism" (as Paul calls it), is not given to all; nevertheless, all are exhorted to strive for the highest charisms (cf. 1 Cor 12:31; 14:1). According to the Apostle to the Gentiles, celibacy for the sake of the kingdom of heaven promotes the total gift of self to Christ and testifies to faith in the next life (cf. 1 Cor 7:25–40). For then—as Jesus himself declares (cf. Mk 12:25)—there will be no more marrying, but all will lead a life like that of the angels. An insufficient appreciation of celibacy for the sake of the kingdom of heaven is an indication that hope in that "kingdom of the end times" is growing ever weaker.

The example of Christ's love for the Church is authoritative for the apostles. They are the "ones sent" by the Lord and the heirs to his saving mission. The task entrusted to them continues through the apostolic succession in which bishops, priests and deacons share. In the first centuries of Christianity, many ministers of the Church were married, yet they were obliged to practice continence, which went back to the tradition of the apostles. The Church Fathers substantiate this with Saint Paul's advice that continence promotes devotion to God in prayer (cf. 1 Cor 7:5). This practice prepared the way for ecclesiastical legislation on celibacy.

In this connection John Paul II emphasized:

> The will of the Church finds its ultimate motivation in the link between celibacy and sacred ordination, which configures the priest to Jesus Christ the head and spouse of the Church. The Church, as the spouse of Jesus Christ, wishes to be loved by the priest in the total and exclusive manner in which Jesus Christ her head and spouse loved her.... And so priestly celibacy should not be considered just as a legal norm or as a totally external condition for admission to ordination, but rather as a value that is profoundly connected with ordination, whereby a man takes on the likeness of Jesus Christ, the good shepherd and spouse of the Church. (*Pastores Dabo Vobis*, nos. 29, 50)

Benedict XVI too has pointed out the connection between the discipline of celibacy in the Latin Church and the personal example of Jesus Christ, who did not marry, while underscoring the nuptial character of this decision: "It is a profound identification with the heart of Christ the Bridegroom who gives his life for his Bride.... The fact that Christ himself, the eternal priest, lived his mission even to the sacrifice of the Cross in the state of virginity constitutes the sure point of reference for understanding the meaning of the tradition of the Latin Church" (*Sacramentum Caritatis*, no. 24).

Manfred Hauke

10   The fundamental magisterial document
      on priestly celibacy is the encyclical by
      Paul VI. What are the most important
      teachings in it?

Among the prophetic documents by Paul VI—*Humanae
Vitae* (1968), *Marialis Cultus* (1974) and *Evangelii Nunti-
andi* (1975), to recall just a few—is, perhaps first of all,
his encyclical *Sacerdotalis Caelibatus* on priestly celibacy
(1967), which certainly remains the principal teaching of
the Magisterium on the subject.

The document is divided into two parts: the first offers
teaching on the *essence* of celibacy; the second is more of
an exhortation and concentrates on the *lived experience* of
celibacy (priestly formation and life, the painful deser-
tions, the fatherhood of the bishop and the shared responsibility of the lay faithful).

With this encyclical the pope addressed the most common objections that are raised with respect to celibacy:
the assumption that this obligation is unnatural from the
physical and psychological point of view, harmful to the
equilibrium and maturation of the personality, responsible for the dwindling numbers of priests, the very cause
of painful cases of priestly infidelity and a sign of a pes-
simistic view of the flesh and of ritual purity that, by
imposing a serious human solitude, is said to deprive the
Church of priestly witness lived out in a family circle.

The pope, however, does not limit himself to a mere apologia for the centuries-old discipline, but offers a vision of broad theological horizons that is open to future development. He is not frightened by the painful perplexities of the moment, but forcefully affirms: "Priestly celibacy has been guarded by the Church for centuries as a brilliant jewel, and retains its value undiminished even in our time when mentality and structures have undergone such profound change" (no. 1). This is certainly not a question of an imposition from above that is blind and deaf to the objections that are ever more insistently being advanced. The pope focuses on the profound reasons of suitability for "the golden law of sacred celibacy" (no. 3), demonstrating that they are more decisive and stronger than any objection. Indeed, since God is the one who calls men to the priesthood, the encyclical illuminates the demanding charism of celibacy in terms of its nucleus, which is of a theological nature, shifting attention from the aspects connected to the purely human plane to a truly supernatural horizon, that of the "perfection of holiness, which moves the human spirit to admiration, since it finds the resources of the human creature inadequate to account for it" (no. 16).

The central message of the encyclical, therefore, consists of presenting *theological reasons* for the choice of celibacy made by the ministers of God, which then elucidate its manifold suitableness. There are three fundamental meanings of celibacy: christological (nos. 19–25), ecclesiological (nos. 26–32) and eschatological (nos. 33–34). Alongside these is the distinctly anthropological dimension (nos. 50–59), which is supplemented—in the second part of the document—by the spiritual and ascetical meaning (nos. 60–69). Here, in summary form, are the principal teachings regarding these five complementary aspects.

1. The christological dimension

Christ, the Supreme Pontiff and eternal High Priest, was the very first to be a celibate in exercising his new priesthood, thus offering an immediate model and the highest ideal for every ministerial priest who shares in his unique priesthood. The virginity of our Lord signified his total dedication to the service of God and mankind, the expression of his perfect salvific mediation between the Father and the human race. He selected the first ministers of this salvation, inviting them to renounce many things for the sake of a close participation in his demanding apostolic mission. The freer that mission is from ties to flesh and blood, the more perfect it will be. In this light the choice of celibacy has always been regarded as a sign of unstinting love and an incentive to practice charity toward all. The deeper reason for the charism of celibacy, therefore, is certainly assimilation or configuration to the charity and dedication practiced by the Redeemer.

2. The ecclesiological dimension

Every ecclesiological reason for celibacy is derived from the christological motive.

> "Made captive by Christ Jesus" unto the complete abandonment of one's entire self to him, the priest takes on the likeness of Christ most perfectly, even in the love with which the eternal Priest has loved the Church his Body and offered himself entirely for her sake, in order to make her a glorious, holy and immaculate Spouse. The consecrated celibacy of the sacred ministers actually manifests the virginal love of Christ for the Church, and the virginal and supernatural fecundity of this marriage. (no. 26)

In this context, too, the primary reason for celibacy is not functional—in other words, greater freedom and availability for ministry, although these do follow from it—but rather the spousal love of Christ for the Church. The eucharistic dimension of priestly celibacy deserves special mention (cf. no. 29). The life of a priest is indeed completely centered on the ministry of grace, in particular the ministry of the Eucharist, in which the whole Church is reflected and finds all her spiritual good. In consecrating the Eucharist the priest acts *in persona Christi* and unites his life to Christ's sacrifice, offering himself to his Lord.

3. The eschatological dimension

Celibacy makes the priest a sign and a pledge of the next life and a living witness to the fact that all believers should tend toward the glorious fulfillment of the kingdom of God. The choice of celibacy anticipates in some way the reality of the eschatological kingdom, in which there will be no more marrying. "The precious divine gift of perfect continence for the kingdom of heaven stands out precisely 'as a special token of the rewards of heaven,' it proclaims the presence on earth of the final stages of salvation with the arrival of a new world, and in a way it anticipates the fulfillment of the kingdom as it sets forth its supreme value which will one day shine forth in all the children of God" (no. 34).

4. The anthropological dimension

The renunciations connected with celibacy are a very special offering made to the love of Christ, and therefore another part of this choice is one's nature, which must be elevated to its supernatural capacities and to evangelical courage. Celibacy does not go against human nature and does not suppress physical, psychological and emotional needs. The response to the priestly vocation implies "the choice of a *closer and more complete relationship* with the mystery of Christ and the Church for the good of all mankind" (no. 54). Thus celibacy too elevates the whole man and contributes to his maturation and perfection through the practice of self-control, as well as the wise sublimation of his own psyche. This requires the capacity for an authentic love that is open to the highest and fullest fatherhood, the capacity for brotherhood, friendship and tenderness, fortitude, personal discipline, and the control and mastery of the emotions and passions. It is about Christian and human values that nourish those interpersonal skills that enable one to build communion among all men, teaching them to overcome all selfishness, indifference and hostility.

5. The spiritual and ascetical dimension

Formation for celibacy is always, above all, formation of a balanced, strong and mature personality; a personality worthy of a *man of God* (cf. no. 60). It is not surprising therefore that first place must be given to the supernatural means, while harmoniously coordinating nature with grace. Celibacy cannot be separated from a particular asceticism proper to the priest and certainly superior to the discipline required of other believers. To live out one's choice of celibacy faithfully demands spiritual combat, humility and perseverance in fidelity to grace. Only an authentic spiritual life provides the solid basis that makes it possible to persevere in this choice. The celibate priest is indeed someone "who, belonging in a special way to Christ, has in Him and through Him 'crucified the flesh with its passions and desires'" (no. 78). The commitment to celibacy, finally, could not possibly do without a spiritual Marian component, because Mary through her own virginity and maternity is the model of perfect union with Christ (no. 98). A commitment to courageous austerity and intense individual and communal spirituality will allow the priest—with the indispensable help of God—to live a life of celibacy with relative ease and in profound joy of spirit.

Finally, we must emphasize a principle that is clearly approved in the body of the encyclical and is particularly relevant today with respect to special cases of admitting married sacred ministers who belong to non-Catholic churches or ecclesial communities but now want to join the Catholic Church and to exercise ministry. Such cases can never signify a relaxation of the law of celibacy currently in force and must not be interpreted as a prelude to its abolition (cf. nos. 42–43).

In *Sacerdotalis Caelibatus* the pope observes that the theme of celibacy, in the twentieth century as never before, has been examined in depth under every aspect: doctrinal, historical, sociological, psychological, pastoral (no. 5). All this notwithstanding, it seems that Paul VI did not intend to say the last word on the subject, but rather to indicate authoritatively the direction for future efforts—going against the current of the prevailing mentality today—so as to understand better and better the providential value of celibacy: "In this way the bond between the priesthood and celibacy will be seen in an ever improving union, owing to its clear logic and to the heroism of a unique and limitless love for Christ the Lord and for his Church" (no. 25).

His message was not neglected but rather deepened and developed by the Magisterium of his successors, from John Paul II (cf. *Pastores Dabo Vobis*, no. 29) to Benedict XVI (cf. *Sacramentum Caritatis*, no. 24), and also by the valid findings of new historical and theological research and by the joyous witness of the majority of priests.

Krzysztof Charamsa

11 The chief task of the priest is the celebration of the Eucharist. What importance can celibacy have here?

To understand one of the foundational reasons for priestly celibacy, we must highlight its close connection with the Eucharist. Indeed, the priest is not a mere "social worker" who acts in ecclesiastical circles. If that were the case, his celibacy would make little sense. But the priest is chosen first of all to be the minister (servant) of an exalted divine action, the Eucharist. Consequently, as the pope recently recalled, "the priest no longer belongs to himself but, because of the sacramental seal he has received, is the 'property' of God. The priest's 'belonging to Another' must become recognizable to all, through a transparent witness." [1]

Essentially, therefore, the priest is defined by his belonging to God and by his sacramental ministry. This, Benedict XVI again notes, is "the proper framework for understanding and reaffirming, in our day too, the value of sacred celibacy which in the Latin Church is a charism required for Sacred Orders".

The priest is essentially destined to celebrate the Eucharist, in other words, to make present the supreme act of

[1] Address to participants in the conference "Faithfulness of Christ, Faithfulness of the Priest", organized by the Congregation for the Clergy, March 12, 2010.

Christ's self-giving to the Church, his Bride ("Take and eat, all of you, this is my Body . . ."); hence the intrinsic spousal logic of the priesthood, of *undivided* gift and *unconditional* service. This logic cannot remain an element outside the priest, since he is not a mere passive instrument of a divine action. Instead he is called to integrate the spousal character of Christ into his own life; he is called to give Christ, by giving himself to all unreservedly, by identifying with Christ himself. In the Consecration of the eucharistic species, the culminating moment of the whole life of the Church, he in fact acts in the person of Christ, the Head and Bridegroom of the Church. From this perspective it is understandable that priestly celibacy acquires a particular value, allowing the minister to offer to the faithful a coherent sacramental sign.

Benedict XVI, in the first message of his pontificate, at the conclusion of his concelebration with the cardinal electors in the Sistine Chapel on April 20, 2005, observed: "The ministerial Priesthood was born at the Last Supper, together with the Eucharist, as my Venerable Predecessor John Paul II so frequently emphasized. 'All the more then must the life of a priest be "shaped" by the Eucharist', he wrote in his last *Letter to Priests for Holy Thursday* (no.1)." Precisely this "eucharistic shape" of the priest's life makes his celibate state so happily appropriate and substantiates his dedication so that he belongs to the Church with a spousal love, continually stirring up his pastoral charity so that he might serve *all* souls.

This was stressed by Benedict XVI in his apostolic exhortation *Sacramentum Caritatis* (2007): "It is not sufficient to understand priestly celibacy in purely functional terms. Celibacy is really a special way of conforming oneself to Christ's own way of life. This choice has first and foremost a nuptial meaning; it is a profound identification with the heart of Christ the Bridegroom who gives his life for his Bride" (no. 24). The priest is therefore called to celebrate the Eucharist, allowing it to shine forth in his life, which is celibate because it is entirely donated.

Arturo Cattaneo

Emotions and Sexuality

12 Is not celibacy unnatural and therefore the cause of existential crises among priests?

In the debate over celibacy in the past decades, peculiar psychological arguments have been made again and again by laymen. We have become almost accustomed to hearing supposedly enlightened contemporaries saying that it is, after all, unnatural to "renounce" sexuality.

This reasoning is based on a completely erroneous concept of nature. What are they implying? Was Mahatma Gandhi, who, in spite of everything, took a vow that was the equivalent of celibacy, unnatural? Is the Dalai Lama unnatural? And what about people who are unmarried, whether intentionally or because things somehow turned out that way—are they all unnatural?

Every man by nature is endowed with human dignity above all. The idea would never have occurred to the Greeks at the height of their philosophical thought that nature was, in this sense, only the corporeal aspect of man. Certain restricted views and naturalistic reductions came to the fore only much later and logically ended in racist definitions of man, which saw authentic man realized only in a very definite race. The practical consequence of the National Socialist concept of race was that the superior race had to continue in existence; hence propagating it had top priority. Mothers were publicly rewarded for having many children. Against this background it is no wonder that the National Socialists, in the context of their consistent battle against the Catholic Church, discriminated against celibacy as "unnatural" and attempted in the so-called morality trials of 1936–37 to discredit priests and religious publicly as homosexuals or as otherwise sexually misguided.

So it is not difficult to see that the concept of nature in the modern era has been misused ideologically in many ways. "Unnatural!" was the battle cry of totalitarian dictatorships against religion and everything that went along with it. Unfortunately we cannot say that this charge "Unnatural!" is now extinct. The remark made by the playwright Bertolt Brecht in 1955, "The womb from which that crept is still fertile", is no less relevant today.

No serious thinker talks about race anymore, yet the pagan cult of the body has meanwhile had a major revival. Sometimes one gets the impression that by keeping the human body healthy and fit, people are trying to ensure for themselves something like eternal life. The body becomes a status symbol, a way of staging the self in an increasingly narcissistic culture. Sexual activity consequently becomes the decisive criterion for one's own market value. Thus the new cult of the body produces equal-opportunity unhappiness for the millions, because the whole project is necessarily frustrated by the trivial fact that every human being ages. Yet precisely for this reason, a lifestyle like celibacy, which consistently contradicts the absurd dogmas of the prevailing idolatry of the body, is especially provocative.

So without realizing it, people resort to the old Nazi trick and discriminate against celibacy as "unnatural", which implies that they are thereby indirectly declaring themselves and their constantly changing, always unsatisfying sexual relationships as totally "natural". Basically a healthy person at peace with himself could be completely indifferent to whether other people renounce sexuality voluntarily or because of illness or similar reasons. The massive aggression with which such accusations are sometimes hurled, however, is a psychological indication that the aggressor himself could have some sort of problem with his own sex life that he is just unwilling to admit.

The accusation that celibacy is "unnatural" comes also, though, in another variation that is not neurotic at all. This is the "macho version". There are men who rush headlong at the world of women with the cry: "Must. Have. Sex!" As a psychotherapist I would say that someone who cannot control his own sexual urges is not fit for marriage. In a mature marriage, each spouse pays attention also to the needs of the other. There are various reasons why it is not possible in a marriage, temporarily or long-term, for the spouses to express their sexuality in a genital way. From this reality we can arrive at a valid principle: anyone who cannot do without sex is not capable of marriage. The celibate life becomes unnatural only when being single turns into isolated selfishness or narcissistic self-dramatization. But a married person is not immune to this danger either.

Besides the reproach of "unnaturalness", priestly celibacy is often pointed to as one of the chief reasons for certain existential crises of some priests. From my experience as a therapist, I can comment that such crises are not caused by celibacy but rather by the drying up of the spiritual life. If a priest no longer prays regularly, if he himself no longer goes to confession, and if he therefore no longer has a living relationship with God, then as a priest he is no longer productive. People notice that the power of God's Spirit no longer goes out from this man. Obviously all this can lead to frustration and dissatisfaction for the priest in question. In such a situation, if an external relationship offers itself, then the priest is in great danger of allowing the already crumbling dams to be demolished entirely. Someone who practices celibacy like a bureaucrat, during office hours only, will come to grief.

Conversely a vigorous priest who lives out his faith convincingly, as an example to others, is a productive pastor of souls, who can thus take joy in his pastoral work because he is helping people. This occurs especially in hearing confessions. Celibacy frees the priest for intensive pastoral contacts, because it makes it possible for him to devote himself more thoroughly, with regard to both time and personal concern, than if he were married. For psychologically healthy men, celibacy, now as always, means an opportunity to lead an intellectually stimulating and exciting life full of spiritual fruitfulness. And for the Church it is a precious gift of God—for which we of course must constantly pray.

Manfred Lütz

13 Is not the requirement for perfect continence in celibacy harmful to one's psycho-physical equilibrium and to the maturation of the human personality?

It is easy to understand that priestly celibacy is harmful neither to a man's psycho-physical equilibrium nor to the maturation of his personality, if we consider that it is a free, conscious choice of a psychologically mature person. Psychological maturity is essential for someone who wants to respond to a call to the priesthood. By *maturity* we mean the psycho-physical equilibrium, in other words, a successful integration of the intellectual and emotional-volitional components in the personality as a unified whole.

To understand celibacy correctly it is necessary to keep in mind that the sexual dimension, on these three levels (biological, psychological, spiritual), is an essential dimension of the person, and hence even the person who chooses celibacy is profoundly marked by it.

Furthermore it must be emphasized that the sexual dimension cannot be reduced to mere genital activity. A human being is not reducible to a bundle of instincts. As a person, he possesses an intellect, a will and freedom, which make possible effective self-control of his physical, psychological and emotional appetites. The freer a person is, the more he lives out the sexual dimension of his being in a personal way, that is, as an expression of his own spiritual interiority. There is no denying that emotional maturity involves the passage from an ego-centric affectivity, typical of the newborn, to an affectivity that is open to a sacrificial love even unto total self-giving, or spousal love.

Celibacy requires therefore "clear understanding, careful self-control and a wise sublimation of the psychological life on a higher plane" (Paul VI, *Sacerdotalis Caelibatus*, no. 55). In reality this means a process of integrating one's sexuality harmoniously, which gradually leads one to elevate his sexual energies and invest them in a life plan that renounces the exercise of genital sexuality. The more humanly and spiritually mature a person is, the more perfectly he will practice continence at the psychological level, not as frustration but as perfect freedom exercised in self-control and in complete availability to his personal mission.

This is a dynamic process that takes time and interior education, continual vigilance over the heart, which, by means of the virtue of chastity, brings about the integration of the emotions and impulses into a life plan. The virtue of chastity directs the person toward the most perfect gift of self possible according to the state of life he has chosen, whether matrimony or celibacy. It is helpful to recall the interdependence that exists among the various virtues or dispositions of the heart, such as prudence, justice, fortitude. From a theological and spiritual perspective, one cannot deny the importance of the theological virtues and of the gifts and fruits of the Holy Spirit that surpass the limits of mere human nature, which often causes us to experience its ambiguities and our own egotism.

If the maturation of the human personality requires the dimension of interior freedom as well as self-control, then the celibate life is not opposed to that fulfillment of the human personality but, on the contrary, fosters it, as is clear from the example of balanced human development in a great number of men and women who have chosen celibacy. As for psycho-physical equilibrium, perfect continence will be considered as an unbalancing factor only by an outlook that separates the corporeal reality of the human person from his psychological and spiritual dimension, and only in a state in which all the dimensions of a human being are insufficiently integrated. A failure can be the result of abstinence from sexual life that is imposed as part of a repressive outlook on sexuality and not according to a holistic view. Furthermore, failures to integrate sexuality harmoniously into priestly life are not infrequently caused by a sense of frustration or sterility or by a feeling of loneliness resulting from difficulties in relating with one's fellow priests or parishioners.

André-Marie Jerumanis

14 Can the obligation of perfect continence cause sexual and emotional deviance, as well as infidelity, scandals and painful defections that hurt the whole Church?

In all states of life, not only in priestly celibacy but also in marriage, we encounter sexual and emotional deviations. Pedophilia is a recent example of this, as statistics and various scientific studies show. Infidelity is unfortunately a very widespread reality in marriage too. It may seem obvious that moral failures occur in all states of life, yet it is still true that much is expected by believers and by all who, recognizing the educational function of the priest figure, are scandalized by the acts of sexual misconduct committed by some priests. Some maintain that the cause of these calamities is to be found in celibacy. But just as it would be rash to declare that marital crises are due to the requirement that marriage be indissoluble, it would be nonsensical to blame celibacy for the scandals caused by some priests.

It is necessary instead to examine carefully the real causes for priestly infidelity and the inability to remain faithful to a free choice made at a certain moment of one's life. Greater attention to human, psychological and spiritual maturity in the formation of persons who choose celibacy for the kingdom of God is necessary now more than ever, while always keeping in mind that the reality of sin calls for greater attention to the dimension of ongoing personal conversion and therefore to the spiritual life.

We should not underestimate elements that make it difficult to practice celibacy, such as a lack of faith, of love for the Church or of a prayer life; an erroneous concept of sexuality that places the emphasis on biological determinism; physical and psychological fatigue; an excess of visual stimuli (Internet etc.); the abuse of nicotine, caffeine, alcohol and the like; and also dietary imbalances. Other factors should not be overlooked either, such as the failure to heal negative experiences in the past; the attitude of doubt that does not allow the choice of celibacy once and for all, with no possibility of going back; or waiting for a hypothetical change in ecclesiastical law.

When someone thinks of resolving the problems connected with the life of a priest by proposing the abolition of celibacy, it would be helpful to recall the words of the psychoanalyst T. Anatrella: "Marriage has never been a form of therapy for emotional and sexual immaturity."

André-Marie Jerumanis

15   What positive message does celibacy have for today's society?

In the present-day context of secularized culture, celibacy for the kingdom of God is rich in significance. For today's world—which is tempted to close itself off within a this-worldly horizon and to absolutize love for material beauty—love for the absolute beauty of God, which is revealed in the glorious face of Christ, has a strong symbolic value as a signpost pointing to the invisible love of God. It is an invitation to reflect on the folly of those who choose the one love that "alone suffices", God's love. A life lived solely for the sake of this love manifests the presence of God and serves as a powerful witness, an invitation to reflect on the nature of the God proclaimed by Christians, the God of love who is able to supply the need for tenderness in a priestly heart that remains "human".

Freud talks about the positive aspect of Christian celibacy for the society in antiquity, inasmuch as it appreciated the authentic meaning of the love that cannot be reduced to the sensual, transitory aspect of one moment. "In eras when the satisfaction of amorous desire met with no obstacle or difficulty, for example during the decline of the ancient cultures, love came to be deprived of value, life became empty, and there was a need for forceful education in reaction so as to restore the indispensable emotional values to their proper place. In this context it can be said that the ascetical current in Christianity created psychological values for love that pagan antiquity could never had conferred upon it" ("On the Universal Tendency to Debasement in the Sphere of Love", 1912). In this sense, even today, given the signs of a dehumanization of sexuality, celibacy can have a remedial and educational function, inviting contemporaries to overcome either a hedonistic anthropology (a vision of man that essentially prioritizes the pleasure principle) or an anthropology that considers man from a materialistic perspective, so as to promote an anthropology that allows for an integral conception of human sexuality.

The promise of fidelity to the love of God, for one's whole life, is a strong rebuke to all of contemporary society, which is characterized by the fragility of its emotional ties and has been described by Z. Bauman as "a society based on the liquidity of love". Benedict XVI, in his encyclical *Deus Caritas Est*, recalls that full and lasting love is possible only insofar as *eros* and *agape* (ascending love and descending love) meet: "Even if *eros* is at first mainly covetous and ascending, a fascination for the great promise of happiness, in drawing near to the other, it is less and less concerned with itself, increasingly seeks the happiness of the other, is concerned more and more with the beloved, bestows itself and wants to 'be there for' the other" (no. 7).

Celibacy for the kingdom of God helps one to find in the pierced heart of Christ the model and the source of the perfect synthesis of *eros* and *agape* to which every human love should tend, since it is called to be purified and thus led to its true greatness.

André-Marie Jerumanis

16 Does obligatory celibacy foster the presence of homosexuals in the priesthood?

If, in some diocese, one were to observe a relatively high number of priests with homosexual tendencies, the cause could not be the celibacy requirement, for the simple fact that the promise of celibacy presupposes that the future priest is heterosexual. In fact the voluntary and conscious renunciation, for love of the kingdom of heaven, of those natural goods, marriage and family, is possible only for a heterosexual man. If someone were to promise to renounce something that for him is not a natural good but rather indifferent, foreign, or unattractive to him, in reality he would not be giving something up; the term *renunciation* would become absolutely devoid of content and would have no meaning.

Given that, according to Catholic morality, sexual relations are legitimate only within the context of marriage between a man and a woman, a man with homosexual tendencies can promise only what is required of any unmarried Catholic, namely, to practice sexual abstinence; whereas a heterosexual man who agrees to celibacy accepts an obligation that goes much further than that.

In the book-length interview *Light of the World*, Benedict XVI listed the reasons why homosexuals cannot become priests:

Their attitude toward man and woman is somehow distorted. . . . Their sexual orientation estranges them from the proper sense of paternity, from the intrinsic nature of priestly being. The selection of candidates to the priesthood must therefore be very careful. The greatest attention is needed here in order to prevent the intrusion of this kind of ambiguity and to head off a situation where the celibacy of priests would practically end up being identified with the tendency to homosexuality. (pp. 152–53)

If, in some diocese, there were a relatively high number of priests with homosexual tendencies, this would indicate that the criteria for selecting candidates to the priesthood had not been followed carefully enough. But that is another matter, which we will deal with in the next answer.

Peter Mettler

17 What should be done to avoid the spread of homosexuality in the clergy?

This problem must be taken very seriously. Indeed, we are facing today a gradual homosexualization of our whole society, a growing irrationality in this area and a "dictatorship of relativism" pushing toward a policy that is passed off as a model of tolerance but in reality degrades man and tends to establish a climate of moral relativism or indifference. This tends to undermine the structure of values and the roles of the sexes as we have known them until now and which are inspired by the Christian image of man; this creates the presuppositions for a profound change in society with fatal consequences.

In recent years different Vatican dicasteries have published guidelines and documents in which they absolutely forbid the ordination of men who practice homosexuality, have deeply rooted homosexual tendencies or promote the so-called gay culture. These documents alone are not enough. Those responsible for admitting candidates to the priesthood must first of all be willing to see the problem inherent in seminarians and clerics with homosexual tendencies and to confront it with a specific plan, calmly and with determination. It is absolutely counterproductive to ignore this problem, to minimize it or simply to wait, in the hope that it will resolve itself, as is sometimes done.

One indispensable prerequisite is that, apart from any ideology, seminary staff members strive to acquire a deep pastoral competence in this particular area and to accept Christian doctrine pertaining to homosexuality as it has repeatedly been explained and confirmed in various declarations of the Magisterium. They must avoid confronting this problem reluctantly by relegating it unilaterally to the internal forum, given that this is an essential point pertaining to the suitability of the candidate to the priesthood. From the moment of his admission to the seminary and his acceptance for the conferral of orders, it is necessary for the seminary staff to proceed with great diligence and consistency, without allowing themselves to be affected by the desire to increase the number of vocations. Quality is more important than quantity.

This approach would allow the authorities to clear off at the outset, to a great extent, the terrain that lends itself to the spread of homosexual subcultures and networks, which arouse feelings of repulsion in heterosexual candidates and not infrequently lead them to abandon the path to the priesthood.

Homosexuality should be explicitly declared an impediment to ordination and included as such in the pertinent canonical norms. More than documents from Vatican dicasteries, such a law would better highlight, in an unambiguous way, the necessity and the importance of such a rule. But even more decisive will be the recognition by bishops, priests, theologians and lay faithful of the fullness of Christian truth in matters of sexual morality, thus contributing to a renewal both of the priesthood and of marital and family life.

Peter Mettler

18 Is celibacy the cause of sexual abuse on the part of some priests?

The latest media exposés about sexual abuse—and in particular about pedophilia—in clerical circles are being taken by some as an occasion to point their finger at celibacy. This alleged connection has nevertheless been refuted point by point by experts and has been declared absolutely arbitrary and untenable.

Really, in light of the current situation, there should be no need for any further explanations. No one, for example, would ever dream of blaming marriage for the fact that a parent commits pedophilic crimes. Such crimes are a monstrous aberration and are neither justified nor fostered by any Christian family status. They are as foreign to the human person as they are to love. And anyone who marries or chooses to remain unmarried for the sake of the kingdom of heaven does so out of love.

Unfortunately, though, a devastating judgment about the sexual conduct of the Catholic clergy has become firmly rooted in the perception of the public. For a long time now, many ecclesiastical discussions among users of the interactive media are accompanied by a litany of positively contemptuous and insulting remarks about priests. Surely many of these commentaries in the blogs arise within the context of pubertal emancipation from religion or are the expression of pathological forms of aggression and resentment. Nevertheless they substantially reflect society's view of the Catholic Church. When the clerical abuse scandal reached its height in the United States in 2002, 64 percent of the participants in an opinion poll stated that Catholic priests would certainly abuse children regularly (*Wall Street Journal–NBC News*, April 2002).

Aside from these and similar prejudices, as well as certain campaigns to destroy the reputation of the Church and of priestly celibacy, the question remains whether celibacy could in fact be the cause of the horrible crime of child abuse among priests.

Other essays in this volume deal with the psychological aspects of this question. Therefore my intention here is only to show that an analysis of the available data on this phenomenon clearly proves that there is no connection whatsoever between celibacy and the aforementioned cases of abuse.

The coverage and attention that the accusations of abuse received in the United States over the past decade also brought to light many observations that can be helpful in answering this question. According to the *Washington Post* (June 9, 2002) and the *New York Times* (January 12, 2003), the number of priests accused of sexual crimes against children and adolescents range between 1.5 and 1.8 percent of all the priests who were ordained between 1950 and 2001. Professor Philip Jenkins of Pennsylvania State University, in his study *Pedophiles and Priests*, calculates that between 0.2 and 1.7 percent of priests are pedophiles. Three-quarters of one percent of priests currently ministering in the United States are facing accusations of abuse (*Star Tribune*, July 27, 2002). In Europe a few less-detailed statistics are available. The abuse scandal in Ireland that convulsed the Church in 2009 extends as far back as the 1930s. Sexual abuse is only one aspect of it, since the commission that was established to review the past deals above all with emotional abuse and the use of corporal punishment, the questionable application of which for pedagogical purposes is less a reflection on specific Catholic practice than on the general educational ideas of the time.

More telling with regard to the problem of sexual abuse are the statistics from Germany. In reaction to media reports, which had singled out the Diocese of Rottenburg-Stuttgart as being especially affected, the diocese published a statement (*kath.net*, February 16, 2010). Since 2001 there had been twenty-three suspected cases of abuse involving both priests and lay coworkers. In eleven cases there was credible evidence of illegal conduct. Six of these cases had occurred in the past, sometimes decades before, and the accused had already died. The criminal proceedings in the remaining five cases resulted in acquittal and the imposition of fines, which, however, were paid without any admission of guilt. Pro-rated against the total number of pastoral coworkers, the proportion of culprits would be somewhere in the tenths of a percent.

In Italy, which presently has more than fifty thousand priests in ministry, eighty priests in the last decade (*Zenit*, February 2, 2010) have come under suspicion of sexual abuse or have been convicted. If this figure is compared with the number of priests who have done pastoral work during the last ten years, the rate of sexual criminals in the clergy is somewhat more than 0.1 percent. It is to be feared that the cases that went unreported because of social connections would increase this rate significantly, but a total greater than comparable figures in other countries is in any case unlikely. So much for statistics on the Catholic clergy.

While the media reports about the abuse scandal among the Catholic clergy in the United States were reaching their climax, the *Christian Science Monitor* (April 5, 2002) published a relatively unnoticed national study by the inter-denominational institution Christian Ministry Resources, according to which the Protestant churches in North America could be affected by cases of abuse at even higher rates than the Catholic Church and that, among the persons accused, the percentage of volunteer coworkers was greater than that of the official employees and pastors. In his book, Philip Jenkins cites an investigation that found that from 2 to 3 percent of pastors from Protestant institutions face the accusation of sexual abuse. Even though it is always advisable to treat such numbers and statistics with caution, the numbers nevertheless should be roughly accurate, as a 2007 report by three North American insurance firms suggests. Together they insure about three-quarters of all Protestant congregations against claims for damages, and they record about 330 cases of abuse annually, with only slight variations over the last few decades.

Although, with child abuse, even more sinister statistics are always to be feared and deplored, according to the reported cases the number of instances of abuse by Protestant pastors is greater than that by the Catholic clergy. The much greater media attention given to reproaches against the Catholic Church can be explained by many factors. Not to be overlooked, however, is the fact that as a uniform corporate body that is universally widespread, the Catholic Church is potentially within the experience of almost everyone and thus has relevance in the media everywhere. Whereas sexual abuse by American Catholic clerics was widely reported and discussed even in Europe, the case of a Lutheran pastor in Texas, for example, whose countless victims were awarded $69,000,000 in damages, would be unknown to most people.

When the picture is widened to include more than just church workers, one finds further sad and disturbing statistics. Charol Shakeshaft, who did research commissioned by the United States Department of Education, suspects that 15 percent of all students are confronted, before they attain majority, with sexual misconduct by a teacher.

This data makes the pressing problem of sexual violence against children and minors all too clear. Furthermore, according to various studies, by far the largest segment of perpetrators of sexual crimes comes from the victims' immediate family circle. In the last fifteen years in Germany, approximately 210,000 cases of child abuse were reported to the police. About one hundred (*Der Spiegel*, February 2010) of these cases are said to have involved Catholic clergy.

For criminal psychiatrist Hans-Ludwig Kröber, priests are therefore involved in cases of abuse at below-average rates. Men who do not practice celibacy, according to Kröber, are thirty-six times more likely to become child abusers (Catholic News Agency, February 7, 2010).

This statistical perspective on the phenomenon, needless to say, in no way changes the fact that sexual abuse by Catholic clergy is especially horrible, tragic and offensive, because of the dignity bestowed on a priest of Christ. Another especially aggravating factor seems to be the shortcomings of various ecclesiastical authorities in dealing with accusations, as well as the attempt to solve the problems merely by transferring accused priests. Admittedly, it is not always easy to determine the facts of the case. Moreover there have in fact been numerous baseless accusations.

Then there is another problem. Most cases of child abuse by Catholic clergy are not the result of pedophilia, but rather of homosexual ephebophilia directed at postpubertal teenagers. Between 1970 and 1980, it was the

current scholarly opinion in psychiatry that an ephebophile priest, unlike a genuine pedophile, could be assigned
again to a pastoral position after successfully completing
therapy. And so the bishops were advised accordingly by
their psychological experts. All these remarks are by no
means supposed to belittle the problem, much less to deny
it. Both pedophile and ephebophile priests inflict hor-
rific suffering on children or minors and great harm on
the Church.

Precisely for this reason it is absolutely urgent today to
recognize the problem clearly and to deal with it trans-
parently, as the pope and an ever greater number of bishops are indeed doing. The fact that in many places
appropriate reporting procedures and commissions have
already been set up is to be applauded. On the other
hand, where there is remedial work to do, immediate
action should be taken. At any rate, in training future
generations of priests, greater attention will have to be
paid to signs of sexual disturbances and pathological inclinations. It should never be permitted to sweep such deeds
under the rug or to overlook them.

In conclusion, it should be noted that according to
the available data child abuse is not a specifically clerical
problem—and certainly not a problem of Catholic clergy
in particular. Therefore a debate about celibacy and ecclesiastical sexual morality is nothing more than ideological
trench warfare that misses the real problem. Many interest groups are all too happy to blame "wicked Rome"
and to use it as a scapegoat. But this exploitation of the
victims too is ultimately a form of repression and not a
way of coping with the guilt.

Johannes Maria Schwarz

Discerning and Fostering a Vocation

19 Is it possible to ask young people today to commit themselves to celibacy for the sake of the kingdom of heaven?

Before addressing this question, we should reflect on the situation of the adolescent or of the young man who stands at the threshold of maturity at the end of his education.

In January 2008 Pope Benedict XVI wrote a letter to his diocese and to the city of Rome in which he spelled out the inevitable conclusion to be drawn from reflection on the "educational emergency" in a society with a predominantly relativistic culture. Where the light of truth has been diminished and the fundamental values of human life seem to fluctuate in an existential tide with no fixed shoreline, "every person is in fact condemned to doubting the goodness of his or her own life and the relationships of which it consists, the validity of his or her commitment to build with others something in common."[1]

It goes without saying that in this atmosphere, which entails the interior corruption of the human person, the very structure of a youth's personality is marked by fragility and indecisiveness in confronting the basic choices of life.

[1] Address to the participants in the Ecclesial Diocesan Convention of Rome on "The Family and Christian Community", June 6, 2005.

The panorama is further complicated when it is a question of the relation between the person and love, since this is the factor that brings human life itself to recognize that it is structurally a "relation", a rapport with another, a need for the other. Today, unfortunately, the person in all his interior dynamics, and in the expressions pertaining to emotional life and the body, is to a great extent missing as a primary concern from the educational curriculum. Young people are tempted to satisfy their instinctive needs; sexuality is thought of in crude terms as a bodily explosion, rather than as a language in which the human person expresses himself in his emotional capacity, specified by the masculine/feminine dimension. Therefore a formidable doubt arises: if these are the circumstances, and they are certainly discouraging, how can we still propose the choice of celibacy to the boys or youths of today?

The central point, it seems to me, should not be the proposal of celibacy (at least not initially), but rather a concern for the education of the human person as a whole. If the boy or youth is not introduced from the beginning to a reasoned and passionate understanding of the reality that he is experiencing, it will be very difficult for him to view celibacy as a satisfying option that makes love possible as *love for the person.*

When Jesus gave his disciples challenging teachings about the costs of following him, and they questioned him about these, the Master responded, "Not all men can receive this precept, but only those to whom it is given.... With men this is impossible, but with God all things are possible" (Mt 19:11, 26). The superhuman standard proposed by Christ is not always that easy to accept, but it is no less human because of that. On the contrary, it is a standard of superabundant love, which mobilizes reason, will and freedom.

What can be done to make giving up possessions and family life in order to embrace the priesthood of Christ a goal that today's youth will consider worthwhile? It seems to be a reasonable proposal only as part of an intelligent, disciplined formation program that helps young men to read and to interpret satisfactorily their basic experiences: feelings, emotions, urges, inclinations. These experiences are often chaotic and incoherent and need to be addressed with the help of a mentor/teacher who can explain their full significance, patiently assisting the young person so that he can come to know and understand himself.

Only in such a context, patiently rebuilding the foundation, can a plan to give one's life to God ripen. In other words, seeing one's humanity being formed to be given to Christ as the natural result of a desire for the fullness of a life spent for the Church and for one's brethren.

In this regard Jesus' meeting with the rich young man is significant. That youth approached Jesus and asked him about the good that he had already started to develop and had taken to heart: "What must I do to have everlasting life, life in its fullness?" Only upon further reflection did the young man realize that Christ's plan was too demanding for him. But he had arrived by himself at the threshold of the question and at the need for an answer, perhaps by a natural desire for good that had been instilled in him by his family upbringing or that came from a tradition of his community.

Today, unfortunately, young men do not even arrive at the threshold of the question, perhaps due to their lack of experience in searching for the ultimate meaning of life.

A youth today can be compared to the paralytic at the pool of Bethsaida, who lay beside the reservoir of healing waters but unfortunately had no one to lower him into the pool at the right time. Many young men have no adult person in their lives who can lead them to the water, that is, awaken in them the slumbering question about human fulfillment.

My experience suggests that where there are communities in which the fabric of interpersonal relationships is produced by a vision of life that places the person at the center of that community's path of salvation, in which the values being proposed are actually confirmed by real firsthand experience, there are almost always vocations, young people dedicating themselves to God. The choice of celibacy becomes a decision following logically from one's personal availability, so that that beauty of a life lived generously can continue and develop fully.

Ernesto William Volonté

20 How can the beauty and value of celibacy be presented to someone who wants to become a priest?

With each passing year I am more convinced that there are no magic formulas in the field of educating and training young people for a human life. It is a matter of understanding clearly where you are going, knowing the destination so as to take the right steps. Besides that, one needs an adequate language—in other words, an approach to the person that keeps together all of the factors that are in play: intellect, emotions, passions, a wholesome climate of interpersonal relationships and reflections on actual experiences.

Hence the decisive point is to return continually to the original human source, that is, to the person in all his richness, to the *humanum*, the beginning of every authentic life of self-giving that grace will bring to its fulfillment. As with every person, the crucial thing is to propose the firm connection between human nature and divine grace.

1. First of all, there needs to be the adventure of a great love. Pedagogically, in practical formation, it is necessary to give the experience of interpersonal relationships priority over the experience of service and ministry. Without the experience of a great love, service tends to give way to the functional or administrative aspect. This is plainly taught by the marital dynamic: the exclusive

love for a particular man or woman is what includes the irrevocability of love: "I will love you alone forever." The particularity of love, as in a true friendship, is what makes a person available to serve the life of another in imitation of Christ.

2. If the priest is committed to being conformed to Christ, the Beloved, then he will affirm his true task in the presence of the Christian people, without half measures. If someone were to speak to me about it, I would say, "Ask me for nothing but to teach you not to prefer anything to Christ and not to adopt the ways of this world." The future priest who is psychologically immersed in this dynamic will form a habitual attitude of comparing everything with Christ's way of being, leading progressively to an identification with him. The candidate for the priesthood, situated in that interior tension between intellect, will and freedom, is thus formed to confront reality (even the most minute everyday details) with an ability to judge and interpret real things according to an authentically Christian spirit.

3. The body itself is one of the signs that expresses the priestly personality. To the young man who knocks at the door of the seminary, it is necessary to speak about the meaning contained in the sign of the body. A formation that considered the bodily reality only in its physical, biological aspect (thereby inculcating, above all, a moral guardianship that never manages to develop the symbolic dimension of the body) would situate the body essentially in a regimen of efficient functioning instead of in the dimension of self-gift for the sake of an ideal (cf. Heb 10:7).

It is possible, however, to give one's own body—which is the manifestation of an undivided interior life—only in a unique, irrevocable and fruitful relationship.

Outside of those parameters of meaning, the body is deprived of the value attributed to it in the order of the Redemption.

Patiently proposing this level of educational discourse to a young man will decisively challenge his freedom and will guard him against all voluntaristic or moralistic impulses and lead him back, in an intensive, critical discussion, to his real or presumed personal relationship with Christ and with the Church.

For these reasons, celibacy practiced with this awareness can be a beneficial drug for the modern era, an era in which the human body has become predominantly a commodity for trade and is no longer the gift of self in love. Thus, in this inconsistent contemporary context, celibacy comes to assume a high cultural profile, as an antidote to the decline of the person to the status of a functional thing.

It adds savor to life, this noble awareness of their own human destiny which future priests must realize in order to be celibate, not giving in to a view of celibacy as a debilitating and repressive state. Virginity for the kingdom of heaven and a hundredfold recompense already here and now—together with hostility of every sort (cf. Mk 10:29)—is not a heavy and almost insupportable burden imposed by the Church for the sake of pastoral work.

Ernesto William Volonté

21 How does one discern a call to the celibate life?

One can be faithful to the choice of a life entirely dedicated to Christ and the Church only if that choice fills one's mind, heart and life. Obviously this does not exclude sacrifice, but rather requires a certain strength of character and decisiveness in order to avoid or to defend oneself against anything contrary to that choice once made. Nevertheless, ethical effort alone will not repel the fiery arrows of everyday circumstances, unless there is, above all, an openness of the emotions and of the intellect to the meaning and ultimate significance of the choice that has been made. The quality of the choice, however, needs to be developed continually. Romano Guardini, who was a theological and pedagogical genius, expressed the foundation of it this way: "In the adventure of a great love, everything in its order becomes an event." In other words, every aspect of life is recognized as a freely given opportunity that the person freely accepts, aware that what he is experiencing is something new and unheard of. Thus every circumstance becomes a proposition for life, challenging it, correcting it, sustaining it, and opening it up to the future.

Hence the formative path in the seminary, in its overall educational approach, must tend to create a climate conducive to the adventure of a great love for Christ and for the Church, for our brethren and for the persons we meet.

This is true also for marriage, since the human dynamics that lead to the choice to marry or to embrace celibacy are identical: one becomes totally dedicated to Christ in the same way that one falls in love. It is very difficult for a man to lose his head over another woman if he continually nourishes and renews the adventure of a great love with his wife. Only in this way are even the everyday routines of life permeated with the atmosphere of the satisfying event to which one remains faithful forever.

A future priest who does not have this openness of heart and feeling does not have the cards necessary to play the exalting hand of the total gift of self to the ideal. A mediocre, shriveled human existence, which is excessively bent on its own fulfillment but unwilling to throw open the doors to a great human adventure, would be a recipe for failure in the dedicated life of celibacy.

Those responsible for seminary formation therefore should be experts in humanity, acute investigators and promoters of emotional growth in this adventure. Whenever they do not identify in a young man at least the essential prerequisites of this interior dynamism, they must not allow the candidate to advance on the path to the priesthood.

We could repeat here the understandable objection that the first disciples made to the Lord (although in that context they were talking about marriage, it applies even more to priestly celibacy): "If such is the case ... it is not expedient" to choose celibacy. "Not all men can receive this precept," Jesus replied, "but only those to whom it is given" (Mt 19:10–11).

Certainly the value of celibacy is comprehensible only within a context of faith and not from the perspective of a dull, worldly mind-set; its meaning lies in the "something more" that Christ asks of anyone who wants to abide forever with him in a relationship of total self-giving. Otherwise the priesthood would lack something that is *indispensable* and not just *appropriate*. For centuries the Latin Catholic Church has been conscious of this level of reality in celibacy and untiringly preserves this way of being human that is more in conformity with the will of Jesus, the Lord.

Ernesto William Volonté

22 Celibacy is a charismatic gift. How can it be imposed by law?

Certainly celibacy is a charismatic gift and, as such, cannot be imposed by anyone. The Church—guided by the Holy Spirit—has, in fact, gradually recognized the importance of choosing candidates for the priestly ministry from among those who have received this gift. With regard to its value, Jesus explained: "Not all men can receive this precept, but only those to whom it is given" (Mt 19:11). This implies an understandable prudence in discerning vocations to the priesthood. It is in the Church's best interests to prevent a man from becoming a priest if he is not capable of fulfilling the demands of celibacy. It is indeed a gift, but also a task and a call to love more, as has already been stressed in the preceding answers.

On closer inspection, the critique aimed at the Church— that she is trying to impose a charism by law—presupposes an opposition between freedom and obedience as well as between charism and institution. In the Church founded by Christ and animated by his Spirit, such antitheses do not exist.

With respect to the first opposition, it should be noted that the teaching of Christ and his own life show the coexistence and harmony between full freedom and equally complete obedience to the will of God the Father: an obedience that is a free choice to abide by the Father's will. Turning to the Jews who had believed in him, Jesus said: "If you continue in my word, you are truly my disciples, and you will know the truth, and the truth will make you free" (Jn 8:31). It is understandable why gospel freedom is rooted in fidelity to the word of Jesus and therefore in obedience. Freedom to follow Jesus presupposes the choice to remain faithful, which at first glance could seem in opposition to freedom, if freedom is understood—as unfortunately often happens today—simply as the free will to do what one likes. Given such an idea of freedom, it is not surprising that celibacy should be seen only as an unacceptable limit or constraint.

In the predominant culture today there is a tendency to think of freedom as an attempt to elude any binding tie, and from such a perspective it is certainly difficult, if not impossible, to understand the meaning and value of a freely chosen commitment to dedicate oneself not only to the celibate life but also to an indissoluble marital covenant.

The presumed but false opposition between the freedom of a charism and the obligatory character of the law can be unmasked also by considering the complementary roles of charism and institution in the Church.

In this regard it is necessary to keep in mind that the action of the Spirit and that of Christ are complementary. Indeed, the twofold mission of the Son and the Spirit is not only found in the Church's origin, but continues to define her life. In the Church therefore the institution is not a mere allotment of competencies and offices, but rather the context within which the manifold action of the Spirit emerges. The ecclesial institution, constituted chiefly by baptism, confirmation and holy orders, is open to charisms, as can be observed particularly in the hierarchical ministry, the genuine fulcrum of the ecclesial institution.

Joseph Ratzinger has highlighted this charismatic dimension of the sacred ministry, recalling that the latter is actualized principally by a call from God. It follows that "the Church cannot simply of herself appoint 'officials' but has to wait on God's call."[1] We can understand then Jesus' exhortation to pray "the Lord of the harvest to send out laborers" (Mt 9:38) and how the call of the Twelve was the result of a night spent by Jesus in prayer (cf. Lk 6:12–16).

This elucidates also the Church's decision to link this ministry to the personal charism of celibacy. Some have requested the abolition of this link, but Ratzinger denounced therein the tendency to understand sacred ministry "purely as an office that can be assigned by the institution itself. If you want to take priesthood so entirely under your own management, with its accompanying institutional security, then the link with the charismatic aspect found in the demand for celibacy is a scandal to be removed as quickly as possible."[2]

Arturo Cattaneo

[1] "Ecclesial Movements and Their Place in Theology", in *New Outpourings of the Spirit: Movements in the Church*, edited by the Pontifical Council for the Laity, 1999 (San Francisco: Ignatius Press, 2006), p. 23.

[2] Ibid., p. 24.

Celibacy in the Life of a Priest

23 Does not celibacy tend to cause loneliness and frustration in the life of a priest?

The gift of celibacy, accepted for the right motive, that is, dedication to Christ and to souls, not only is not a cause of loneliness but is productive of companionship and friendship—first of all with Christ, who is encountered daily in the Eucharist and in prayer, and then with one's brethren also. The priest learns from Jesus to love rightly and authentically the faithful who are entrusted to his care, without yielding to any sort of possessive temptations, but always spurred on by the desire to serve. As Saint Paul wrote to the Hebrews, the priest "chosen from among men is appointed to act on behalf of men in relation to God" (5:1).

Hence celibacy does not mean inhibiting the heart, which by its very nature tends to love, but is in fact a stimulus to love even more and better, being open to all, without showing preferences that are easily dictated by personal, selfish complacency. In his first encyclical, John Paul II noted that "man cannot live without love. He remains a being that is incomprehensible to himself, his life is senseless, if love is not revealed to him, if he does not encounter love, if he does not experience it and make it his own, if he does not participate intimately in it" (*Redemptor Hominis*, no. 10).

Along the same lines, Paul VI had already observed that priestly celibacy "gives the priest a limitless horizon, deepens and gives breadth to his sense of responsibility—a sign of mature personality—and inculcates in him as a sign of a higher and greater fatherhood, a generosity and refinement of heart which offer a superlative enrichment" (*Sacerdotalis Caelibatus*, no. 56). Thus the priest will be a man rich in humanity, sensitive to the needs of others and not motivated by gratification and approval. As in all respects, his model always remains Christ, who cultivated ties of deep fraternal affection with the persons he met and sought.

It is necessary, however, to keep in mind that the priest, as a "man of God", will necessarily experience a "certain loneliness", above all in the present-day context of widespread secularization, which is gradually excluding God from the public square. Consequently, as Benedict XVI recently pointed out, "the priest often appears 'foreign' to the common perception. This is precisely because of the most fundamental aspects of his ministry, such as, being a man of the sacred, removed from the world to intercede on behalf of the world and being appointed to this mission by God and not by men (cf. Heb 5:1)." [1]

Nonetheless it is also logical that in the life of the priest there should be more difficult moments in which he may feel lonely, as also happens in the life of so many people. In some cases this can be due to health problems, misunderstandings, one's own character flaws and those of others, calumnies or humiliations that can produce a sense of frustration. Therefore the Second Vatican

---

[1] Address on March 12, 2010, to participants in the conference "Faithfulness of Christ, Faithfulness of the Priest", organized by the Congregation for the Clergy.

Council and various other magisterial documents have recalled the importance of cultivating a filial relationship with the bishop and brotherhood with the other priests in the diocese, as well as friendship with the lay faithful who are active in the parishes and may possibly be of assistance in overcoming such difficult moments. This was stressed by Benedict XVI in his book-length interview *Light of the World*, in which he recalled that "priests must support one another and must not lose sight of one another. That bishops are responsible for this, and that we must beg the lay faithful also to help support their priests" (p. 36).

It must also be noted, however, that for the priest the right dose of solitude should not be seen so much as a source of difficulties, but rather as a precious opportunity to create the climate that is indispensable for recollection and prayer, after the example of Jesus, who was able to withdraw often to pray alone. The priest's solitude therefore will not be frustrating but fruitful, because it is irrigated by the presence of Jesus, who in the light of the Spirit puts us in contact with the Father. In this sense, solicitude for silence and the search for places and times in which to remain "alone with the Lord" are necessary for the interior life of the priest and for the fruitfulness of his pastoral ministry. Hence he will be able to say with Saint Ambrose: "I am never so little alone as when I am alone."

Clearly, then, the real danger for the priest is not so much loneliness as it is activism, which tends to leave him interiorly empty. This may prove true at a time when his multiple pastoral and organizational commitments absorb almost all his energies, preventing him from cultivating his own spiritual life. He will have to force himself, therefore, to find those moments of solitude, of recollection, in which to seek intimacy with God in prayer and in meditation on his word.

In order for his pastoral activity to be always a source of satisfaction, it must be nourished continually by his relationship with Christ, who is encountered in prayer and in the sacraments. Action springs then from charity and leads into God's work, which precedes and surpasses us.

If a feeling of depressing loneliness and discouragement has made inroads into the life of a priest, the cause therefore should not be sought in celibacy per se, but rather in the manner in which it has been accepted and then lived out. Unfortunately there are also cases in which those responsible for priestly formation have failed to make a prudent evaluation of the candidate's qualities, but this was already discussed in previous answers.

Arturo Cattaneo

24 Celibacy demands great self-denial. Is it really necessary?

Considering celibacy exclusively as a form of self-denial is a one-sided, distorted view of reality. It would be just as false to consider marriage as a renunciation by pointing out that to marry one woman is to renounce all the others. In both cases it is a matter of making a preferential choice. In the case of celibacy, this choice is defined by the awareness that one can perceive and correspond with the love of God in such a way that it is to be preferred over any other possible loving relationship. Saint Teresa of Avila expressed this in the famous remark: "God alone suffices", in the sense that only God is capable of satisfying all our aspirations. A journalist once asked Cardinal Joachim Meisner, archbishop of Cologne, Germany, whether the Church should change the discipline concerning priestly celibacy after the death of John Paul II, and he replied by asking a question of his own: "Do you think that after John Paul II God will lose heart?"

Part of the vocation to the priesthood is the grace to be able to consider not so much the effort required to make the renunciation as the greatness and beauty of the gift and the mission that are received. Indeed, the priest is called to be the living instrument of Christ's salvific action as the Bridegroom of the Church. Certainly the priest will always have to keep the precious gift of celibacy in a vessel of clay, so to speak. It is fragile, especially if he does not fortify his heart at the purest streams of living water and neglects intimacy with Jesus.

In saying this I do not mean to deny that sometimes the commitment to celibacy may be costly, just as marital fidelity may now and then cost a husband something, but for many reasons it is worth the trouble!

It must be remembered therefore that the priest, in giving up certain physical expressions of love, certainly does not renounce love. On the contrary, from the perspective of faith, the celibate is someone invited to love *more*, to love as Jesus loved, and he will never be without the grace of God, which will enable him to remain faithful to his commitment for his whole life.

Hence celibacy should be considered primarily a joyous and confident affirmation (as Josemaría Escrivá often used to say) of a man who entrusts himself to God and places himself fully, body and soul, at the service of souls.

Arturo Cattaneo

25 Since most lay people are married, would a priest not understand them better if he himself were married?

I do not think so, because a zealous priest has even more life experience than many married people. A married minister or therapist always runs the risk of unconsciously projecting experiences from his own marriage onto the case at hand and acting them out. For this reason, he needs supervision as a rule, so as to avoid that.

In contrast, a good priest has a wealth of experience with many, many marriages. And he can then draw on that for certain difficult cases. This explains the pastoral sensitivity and surprising fruitfulness of the writings of Pope John Paul II about marriage.

Above and beyond that, normal friendships are also important in order to stay grounded. Celibacy should not result in a hermit-like existence. Saint Augustine considered it advisable for celibate priests to live in a house together. Such a household, which is also a spiritual community, provides more opportunities for the necessary *fraternal correction*, well-intentioned criticism, which keeps one from losing touch with reality than some marriages provide. Thus it is clear that celibacy does not really mean solitude, but rather freedom and availability for people and for a special task.

Therefore, in order to tell whether a candidate is suitable for the priesthood, one should find out, among other things, whether he is capable of reading other people, whether he shows cordiality toward others and takes an interest in the lives and sufferings of others. A candidate would very surely be unsuitable if he is exclusively self-centered, if he manipulates and uses others for his own advantage, and if he is overly offended by criticism and perhaps erupts into an uncontrolled, narcissistic tantrum.

One other thing should be mentioned briefly in this connection: in her book on the single life (*Single-Dasein*), the psychoanalyst Eva Jäggi described a person who deliberately lives alone as being especially important even for people who live as couples, since he makes it clear to those people, too, that they are not merely defined by a relationship but have their own value. When a relationship fails—for whatever reasons—it often happens that the person who finds himself alone finds loneliness particularly oppressive. Knowing then that there are people who have voluntarily chosen this state of life gives a person strength and courage in such situations.

Manfred Lütz

26 Would a pastor not fit more easily into a parish community if he were married?

To answer this question we must keep in mind the characteristics of the priestly ministry. If it were to be understood as the role of a mere social worker, one could say that being married could in many cases help or at least would not be a hindrance. But a priest is not a social worker, or more accurately, he is much more than that: he is ordained so as to exercise, in communion with his bishop, the office of Christ the Head and Pastor in the community of believers that is entrusted to him. Moreover Vatican II explained that "while they govern and shepherd the People of God they are encouraged by the love of the Good Shepherd to give their lives for the sheep. They, too, are prepared for the supreme sacrifice" (*Presbyterorum Ordinis*, no. 13).

The priest therefore, with his total gift of self, carries out the ministry of *pater familias*, which, in his pastoral care for a community, fully absorbs him in a communion that is both affective and effective. For the Catholic Church, pastoral ministry involves full-time dedication on the part of the priest, who has to work in evangelization, Christian education and instruction in prayer. He must attend to the spiritual needs of children, youth, the engaged, married couples, the sick and adults who are inquiring about the faith, besides praying with his people, preparing the faithful to celebrate the Christian mysteries and supervising charitable works.

Of course, in all this, the priest must seek the collaboration of the lay faithful, so that they may share the responsibility for evangelization, which is rooted in the priesthood of all the baptized. But the priest is the one who, by virtue of the imposition of hands, his ontological configuration to Christ and his communion with the bishop, is placed at the head of the Christian community to which he is sent, so as to build it up and preside over it.

Vatican Council II underscores that the priest "shares in the authority by which Christ himself builds up and sanctifies and rules his Body" (*Presbyterorum Ordinis*, no. 2). In this sense the whole life of a priest must be aimed at offering his time, his mind and his heart for the family that is the Church, for which the incarnate Word of God gave himself entirely, even unto death on the Cross (cf. Phil 2:8).

To carry out the Father's plan, Jesus Christ set aside his dearest affections and dedicated himself totally to his public life, traveling from village to village with complete availability, to the point where he declared that he had "nowhere to lay his head". The Twelve were his family, whom he called to stay in his company, so that he might then send them to proclaim the good news and to heal, with the authority to drive out demons (cf. Mk 3:15). Jesus of Nazareth did not leave his family so as to form a family for himself according to the flesh, but rather, in his affections, choices and relationships, he practiced total availability so as to "win for the Father" a people that was to be built on conversion and the acceptance of the kingdom of God. For this purpose he chose the Twelve and invited them to stay with him, asking them, as he asked the rich young man (cf. Mt 19:16–22) to leave their own riches. Among these is the legitimate and honest treasure of one's own family according to the flesh, which is renounced so as to devote oneself faithfully and truly to building up the family of the children of God, as we see happening around Jesus.

If one accepts the nature of the priesthood and its pastoral mission in this way, it is understandable that the choice of celibacy has developed in the perspective of a total devotion, by virtue of which a man gives himself away and spends himself totally, with fidelity, vigilance and emotional maturity, so as to edify, sanctify and govern the people of God. This pastoral work requires—as Saint Ignatius of Antioch might say—that a man be entirely "devoured". The minister of Christ is consequently called to follow him also in the complete dedication to which Christ testified when he exclaimed, "Who is my mother, and who are my brethren ... Whoever does the will of my Father in heaven" (Mt 12:48).

Ettore Malnati

Celibacy and Inculturation

27 Is celibacy foreign to our lifestyle?

I would not exactly say "foreign"—celibacy is a provocation. In a world that no longer really believes in a life after death, this way of life is a constant protest against the general superficiality. Celibacy is the constant witness that this world with its joys and sorrows is not everything. There are people who are infuriated by this witness, for it calls into question their own concept of life, and not merely by a paragraph or an off-the-cuff conversation, but by an immensely consequential life-long commitment.

No doubt, if everything was over at death, then celibacy would be idiocy. Why renounce the intimate love of a woman? Why miss out on the touching encounter with one's own children? Why pass up a happy sex life? Only if this earthly life is a fragment that is supposed to find its completion in eternity can celibacy as a way of life shed a bright light on the life that is yet to come. Only then does this way of life loudly proclaim a fullness of life that the yearning of people in every age has glimpsed but was actually revealed to all mankind only when God became man in Jesus Christ, especially through his death and miraculous Resurrection. For our society celibacy acts just like a "thorn in the flesh" that always reminds us, in season and out of season, that the unrelenting concerns and urgent problems of earthly life are not all that matters.

Opponents of celibacy sometimes suggest that celibacy for the sake of the kingdom of heaven would be unobjectionable in a cloister far away from the world. But in the parishes, in the "world", *viri probati*, that is, older (and therefore "proven") men should be admitted to priestly ministry. These are often the same people who would like to dispense with all differences between profane and sacred, including the difference between clergy and laity, between secular and ecclesiastical topics. Of course the belief that God became man is a large-scale irruption of sacredness into the profane sphere. The early Christians realized very clearly that the old pagan concepts of sacred and profane simply could not be carried over into Christianity. There was no longer an abrupt separation. In Jesus Christ, the triune God had drawn the whole world to himself as well. Yet the world was not annihilated thereby; man was not burned up in the presence of the eternal God; time was not dissolved into eternity. The Christians sensed anew that Christianity was "a difference that made a difference", as we would say today in systemic therapy. Christians did not take up a common cause with the world; they perceived themselves as *Ekklesia*, which after all means "called out" of the everyday humdrum routine. But precisely in this way they had their effect on this world without any anxieties about contact with it.

Priests who lead a life that is spiritually motivated and are open to the possibility of art and culture and participate appropriately in the intellectual debates of the day can experience celibacy as a source of particular cultural and spiritual alertness also. So celibacy is admittedly not for weak, anemic characters. Above all it is not for those who are psychologically self-centered and interested only in themselves. The most common problem in selecting men for the priesthood is avoiding not possible sexual abnormalities but rather narcissism, for the vocation of the priesthood is an almost irresistible temptation for some narcissists. To give sermons to other people without fear of contradiction while clad in festive vestments is enticing to some men, but as with other forms of neediness, genuine satisfaction of this desire can never be attained in the priesthood. A priest must have a diametrically opposite mentality. He must, above all, be interested in other people and their needs and make God's glory visible behind the glitter of his own words—not his own meager lights.

Manfred Lütz

28 Does celibacy foster an ecclesial culture that is anti-women and hostile to marriage?

No, I would say it does exactly the opposite: priestly celibacy fosters an appreciation for women and for marriage.

Celibacy for the sake of the kingdom of God transforms the way a priest looks at a woman. A celibate priest looks at her not with covetousness, full of concupiscence, nor with mistrust and the desire to ostracize her, but instead he adopts a new, positive and profoundly appreciative way of looking at her, as Christ does, a look that requires interior maturity and must be consciously cultivated.

John Paul II gives forceful testimony to this: "In order to live as a celibate in a mature and untroubled way it seems particularly important that the priest should develop deep within himself *the image of women as sisters*" (*Letter to Priests for Holy Thursday 1995*). The priest can only be grafted onto the attitude of Jesus himself toward women.

In his *Mulieris Dignitatem*, John Paul II writes: "It is universally admitted—even by people with a critical attitude towards the Christian message—that in the eyes of his contemporaries Christ became a promoter of women's true dignity and of the vocation corresponding to this dignity. At times this caused wonder, surprise, often to the point of scandal: 'They marvelled that he was talking with a woman' (Jn 4:27)" (no. 12). The pope underscored

the fruitfulness of such an attitude, observing in his letter to priests: "If the priest, with the help of divine grace
and under the special protection of Mary, Virgin and
Mother, gradually develops such an attitude towards
women, he will see his ministry met by a sense of great
trust precisely on the part of women whom he regards,
in the variety of their ages and life situations, as sisters
and mothers" (*Letter to Priests for Holy Thursday 1995*).

This is not a matter of falling into a false irenicism, as
though it were no longer necessary to cultivate the virtue of prudence. John Paul II also mentions in his letter
that "the vocation to celibacy needs to be consciously
protected by keeping special watch over one's feelings
and over one's whole conduct", and he adds: "If in a
relationship with a woman the gift and the choice of
celibacy should become endangered, the priest cannot
but strive earnestly to remain faithful to his own vocation." Hence he recalls the importance of the spiritual
life: "Therefore if the priest does not foster in himself
genuine dispositions of faith, hope and love of God, he
can easily yield to the allurements coming to him from
the world."

Priestly celibacy does not mean marginalizing woman
in the work of building up the Church. She is in fact
called, by virtue of the universal priesthood of the baptized to participate, as all the faithful do, in the prophetic, priestly and kingly mission of Christ. The fact
that a woman cannot be ordained a priest cannot be interpreted as a form of discrimination; it would be that indeed
if the ministerial priesthood were a question of power
and not of service. Instead there is a complementarity of
the male mission and the female mission in the Church.
For the Church, "woman as 'sign' is more than ever central and fruitful, following as it does from the very identity

of the Church, as received from God and accepted in faith. It is this 'mystical' identity, profound and essential, which needs to be kept in mind when reflecting on the respective roles of men and women in the Church."[1]

In Christianity the esteem for celibacy for the sake of the kingdom of God is not at the expense of the value of marriage, much less is it a flight from marriage. Both marriage and celibacy are gifts from God. "Each has its own specific charism; each of them is a vocation that individuals, with the help of God's grace, must learn to discern in their own lives" (*Letter to Priests for Holy Thursday 1995*). Each of them is love of a spousal sort, love that is called to make a total gift of self.

In the teaching of Jesus, which is repeated by the tradition of the Church, marriage has its own dignity and sacramental holiness that have been constantly defended for two thousand years. There is however another path for the Christian, a "deliberate choice of celibacy for the kingdom of heaven". Precisely from the perspective of this kingdom there is a complementarity between marriage and celibacy. Faithfulness and fruitfulness characterize both states of life. "Perfect conjugal love must be marked by that fidelity and that donation to the only Spouse (and also of the fidelity and donation of the Spouse to the only Bride), on which religious profession and priestly celibacy are founded" (John Paul II, General Audience, April 14, 1982). The fruitfulness of marriage, too, resembles the spousal love lived out in continence "for the kingdom of heaven", the fruit of which is a spiritual fatherhood or motherhood. We should recall furthermore

---

[1] *Letter to the Bishops of the Catholic Church on the Collaboration of Men and Women in the Church and in the World*, Congregation for the Doctrine of the Faith, May 31, 2004, no. 15.

that celibacy for the kingdom of heaven highlights the transience of this world and the "relativity" of all human emotional ties, as in relative to the love of God, and thus teaches us to love, in the love of our Lord, those persons whom we love on the natural level within the context of marital and familial ties.

André-Marie Jerumanis

29   Is celibacy foreign to non-Western cultures in Africa?

From the beginnings of Christianity on African soil, many young men have responded and still respond generously to the call to the priesthood, so that Africa today is one of the continents that report a rather large increase in the number of priests. In African cultures the values of the Catholic priesthood have in fact found fertile ground that does not resist the characteristic features of priestly life, among them celibacy.

Those who consider celibacy foreign to African cultures stress particularly the importance that African populations assign to children and also the phenomenon of polygamy, which was widespread, above all, in the past and among rural populations. This argument often glosses over or ignores the fact that usually very incidental economic reasons are in play in these situations, thus running the risk of an overly restricted view of culture.

Culture, in contrast, is endowed with a great dynamism that prepares it to respond to man's real, present-day demands in a constant search for what is true, good and just. To maintain that a human value is foreign to a culture is to deny the human beings of that culture the capacity to recognize and respond to what is true, good and just. The prevalence in the African populations of a certain mentality that is unfavorable to celibacy does not preclude the possibility of recognizing and accepting its value in another era, under different circumstances. The question that really needs to be asked is the ancient one that smacks of colonialism: namely, whether the African is essentially a human being in the same way as an American, an Asian or a European is. If he is, he will also be capable of living out the same human and spiritual values, such as celibacy.

On the other hand, it should be recalled that in African cultures there is no lack of appreciation for continence, given that certain religious acts oblige their participants, especially the minister of the religious ceremony, to practice continence, sometimes for a long time. Hence it is not true that Africans are not capable of sexual continence.

Benedict Ejeh

*   *   *

From the religious perspective Africa is profoundly marked by traditional religion. In the culture of that continent, the sacred plays an important role, and there is a widespread conviction that the efficacy of the sacrificial act depends on conditions of moral purity in the one who performs it. For this reason there are those who observe continence in the days preceding the celebration of the rite, and not just then. For example, the high priest of the royal family in southern Benin is obliged to observe perpetual continence from the day of his investiture until his death.

In this context, the celibacy of Catholic priests is perceived as a sign suited to the celebration of the sacraments and the sacramentals. Even though catechists correctly explain that the efficacy of the sacramental action depends solely on Jesus Christ, the conviction remains that the sanctity of the priest (who is appreciated precisely for his moral purity) contributes something more. The chastity of priests is therefore regarded favorably by the people, who are also very demanding with respect to their priests. This is a mentality so deeply rooted in society that it is not uncommon to hear the parents of a priest declare that they too practice chastity so as to support their son's commitment to fidelity. Hence the celibacy of Catholic priests does not pose any particular problems in Africa, although unfortunately there are deplorable cases of infidelity there too.

Occasionally one hears that in Africa it is utopian to demand celibacy of priests, because, among other reasons, it is foreign to the African culture, which is so strongly imbued with the idea of fertility.

The idea of fertility as a sign of fulfillment can indeed make it difficult to understand celibacy as a sign of the kingdom of heaven. However this is not a difficulty in Africa alone. It has been present in all cultures, beginning with the culture of Israel. In African eschatology it is having numerous descendants—the sign of divine blessing—that confers glory to someone who departs from this world.

But why then, despite this perspective, are priestly vocations so numerous in Africa? Obviously God himself is the one who is making inroads into the heart of the cultures. One explanation may be the existence of spiritual fruitfulness. This is not foreign to African culture, as proved by the fact that in the theology of *Vodun*—an African religion that has spread in America also, especially in Brazil and the Caribbean Islands (Haitian Voodoo)—a consecrated man is called *vodunsi* (spouse of the *vodun*). The African term *vodu* means literally "spirit" or "divinity". Thus is expressed a certain fertility of the sacred.

And so the people understand that a Catholic priest, as a consecrated human being, cannot have children, which enables him to be spiritually fruitful.

Édouard Adè

30   Is celibacy foreign to the peoples of India and Latin America?

Throughout India, Catholic priests are generally recognized and respected for their unconditional commitment to serve Christ and the gospel. A celibate is considered somewhat as a representative of God, as a presence of God, inasmuch as he embraces celibacy for love of Christ and the kingdom of God. In this sense the persons of other faiths usually regard positively the celibacy of Catholic priests and the symbolic significance attached to it.

Celibacy was held in great esteem in the church of the Saint Thomas Christians, but when eastern Syria (and Persia) accepted Nestorianism (after the Council of Ephesus in 431), separating themselves from the Universal Church, celibacy too was abandoned by a decree of the Council of Beth Laphath in 484. Thus celibacy was no longer required for the priests of the Saint Thomas Christians. Celibacy became obligatory only under the governance and legislation of the Latin-rite bishops, starting with the Synod of Diamper in 1599. Over the course of history, the two Catholic churches of the Saint Thomas Christians, the Syro-Malabar and the Syro-Malankar, freely and voluntarily adopted celibacy for priestly ordinations, and this is admired and accepted by the members and the priests of the Eastern churches in India.

As far as the appreciation for priestly celibacy among Hindus is concerned, one can say that it is regarded with esteem and reverence. This is so because of our Indian ethos, which sees in celibacy a sign of closeness to God that represents the very presence of God. In Sanskrit the term to express the concept of celibacy is *Brahmacharya*, which literally means "someone who walks, moves, lives in *Brahma* (in God)". The idea of celibacy is central for the ethos of Indian culture.

Indian religious literature is full of praises for single persons and for those who lead a celibate life. Celibacy therefore is not an idea foreign to Indians in their homeland. People in India regard celibates—*sadhus, sants, sannyasis*—with veneration.

It is true that perpetual *Brahmacharya*, or celibacy, is a special vocation, an extraordinary choice. Usually a *pujari*, an Indian priest, is not celibate. There are, however, special cases in which celibacy is an obligatory requirement, for example in order to become priests in particular temples. In the highly religious context of India, it is therefore natural enough to have a great respect for celibate Catholic priests.

To conclude, I can quote a passage from the *Mahabharata* (one of the two great epic poems of India): "Know that in this world there is nothing that cannot be obtained by someone who remains perfectly celibate from birth until death. In a comparison between a person who has knowledge of the four *Veda* and another who is perfectly celibate, the latter is superior to the former who does not follow the celibate life."

Paulachan Kochappilly

* * *

First of all, it is worthwhile to recall that the value of celibacy for the Church in Latin America has constantly been reaffirmed by various general episcopal conferences in full continuity with the teaching of the Universal Church: by the Medellín Conference (1968), the one in Puebla (1979), and also by the latest one held in Aparecida (2007).

The conference in Puebla recalled that priestly celibacy is a sign of a radical commitment, the fruit of a gift that comes from Christ and that guarantees free and generous dedication to the service of mankind (cf. *Puebla Document*, no. 692). The intention was to testify that celibacy frees a man for greater service to others, and hence it is liberty and not an obstacle to the message of integral liberation proposed by the gospel; furthermore it signifies a greater closeness to the poor of all types.

The conference in Aparecida repeated that the configuration of the priest to Christ the Good Shepherd enables him to love God and all mankind with an undivided heart. The growth of hedonism and individualism, which characterizes almost all of the West, prompts us to acknowledge, on the one hand, the need for humility and persevering prayer that God will continue to bestow the gift of celibacy and, on the other hand, an appreciation for the fraternal collaboration among priests.

Sometimes one hears people say that the shortage of priests hinders evangelization and promotes the spread of Protestantism. The growing presence of Protestant communities and the spread of these groups are not, in my opinion, fostered by priestly celibacy. The principal reason for the loss of numbers on the part of the Catholic Church is rather an insufficient commitment among her lay faithful.

Luis Alfredo Anaya

Papal Teachings on the Subject
from Pius XI to Benedict XVI

Papal Teachings on the Subject from Pius XI to Benedict XVI

By His Eminence Cardinal Mauro Piacenza

I will examine some of the most important documents from Pius XI to Benedict XVI, showing the relevance of their teachings and outlining a synthesis. For the sake of brevity I will examine only the most important documents, especially several encyclicals, which prove to be particularly illuminating in this regard.

1. Pius XI and *Ad Catholici Sacerdotii*

Historians have verified the sincere, personal passion of Holy Father Pius XI for priestly vocations and his tireless work for the building of seminaries, throughout the Catholic world, in which young men who were preparing for priestly ministry could receive the appropriate formation.

This is the context in which we should understand the encyclical *Ad Catholici Sacerdotii*, dated December 20, 1935, which was promulgated on the occasion of the fifty-sixth anniversary of the priestly ordination of that pontiff. The encyclical is composed of four parts, the first two devoted more specifically to the "foundations" in

Talk given at a colloquium in Ars on the theme of "Priestly Celibacy: Foundations, Joys, Challenges ...", sponsored by Foyer sacerdotal Jean-Paul II (John Paul II Priestly Association), January 24–26, 2011.

the title (1. "The sublime dignity: *Alter Christus*" and 2.
"Splendid ornament"), whereas the third and the fourth
are more normative or disciplinary in character and con-
centrate on the preparation of young men for the priesthood and on several characteristics of priestly spirituality.

Of particular interest for our topic is the second part
of the encyclical, which devotes an entire paragraph to
chastity. It is located, however, within the second part,
after the paragraph that speaks about the priest as an
"imitator of Christ" and the one devoted to "priestly
piety", thereby showing how Pius XI's concept of the
priesthood was—as the Church still maintains—an ontological, sacramental concept. From this follows the requirement to imitate Christ and the need for excellence in
priestly life, above all with regard to holiness. Indeed the
encyclical declares: "The Eucharistic Sacrifice in which
the Immaculate Victim who taketh away the sins of the
world is immolated, requires in a special way that the
priest, by a holy and spotless life, should make himself as
far as he can, less unworthy of God, to whom he daily
offers that adorable Victim, the very Word of God incarnate for love of us" (no. 35), and also, "since the priest is
an ambassador for Christ (cf. 2 Cor 5:20), he should so
live as to be able with truth to make his own the words
of the Apostle: 'Be ye followers of me, as I also am of
Christ' (cf. 1 Cor 4:16; 11:1); he ought to live as another
Christ who by the splendor of His virtue enlightened
and still enlightens the world" (no. 38).

Immediately before speaking about chastity, as though
to underscore the inseparable bond, Pius XI points out
the importance of priestly piety, declaring: "We mean that
solid piety which is not dependent upon changing mood
or feeling. It is based upon principles of sound doctrine;
it is ruled by staunch convictions; and so it resists the assaults

and the illusions of temptation" (no. 39). Such statements make it clear that the very understanding of sacred celibacy is closely and profoundly related to a good doctrinal formation that is faithful to Sacred Scripture, Tradition and the continual Magisterium of the Church, and also to an authentic practice of piety, which today we might call an intense spiritual life, avoiding all tendencies toward sentimentality (which often degenerates into subjectivism) and also toward the equally widespread rationalistic proclivities that lead to sceptical criticism, which is far removed from an intelligent, constructive critical sense.

In the encyclical *Ad Catholici Sacerdotii*, chastity is described as being closely bound up with piety, "for from piety springs the meaning and the beauty of chastity" (no. 40). Hence there is an attempt at rational justification, according to the natural law, in the statement: "A certain connection between this virtue [chastity] and the sacerdotal ministry can be seen even by the light of reason alone: since 'God is a Spirit,' it is only fitting that he who dedicates and consecrates himself to God's service should in some way 'divest himself of the body'" (no. 42). This first statement, which in our view is a rather weak argument today, in any case connects chastity with ritual purity and consequently would rule out its permanent practice, connecting it with times of ritual worship; this statement is followed by an acknowledgment of the superiority of the Christian priesthood with respect to the priesthood of the Old Testament or the natural priestly institution that is part of every religious tradition.

In this regard, the encyclical centers its reflection on the experience of the Lord Jesus himself, understood as prototypical for every priest. Indeed it declares: "For the Divine Master showed ... high esteem for chastity, and exalted it as something beyond the common power....

All this had almost inevitable consequences: the priests of the New Law felt the heavenly attraction of this chosen virtue; they sought to be of the number of those 'to whom it is given to take this word' (cf. Mt 19:11)" (no. 43).

It is possible to see in these statements from the encyclical a certain complementarity between the intention to base priestly chastity on the requirement of cultic purity and the much broader need (which is better understood today) to present it as *imitatio Christi*, a privileged way of imitating the Master, who lived an exemplary life of poverty, chastity and obedience.

Pius XI does not neglect, however, to cite dogmatic pronouncements regarding the obligation of chastity and, in particular, the Council of Elvira and the Second Council of Carthage, which, although from the fourth century, obviously testify to a previous practice that had been consolidated and therefore could be codified in law.

Striking an unusually modern note (in the sense that it is immediately accessible to our mentality), the encyclical speaks about the freedom with which the gift of chastity is accepted, declaring: "We say 'freely,' for though, after ordination, they are no longer free to contract earthly marriage, nevertheless they advance to ordination itself unconstrained by any law or person, and of their own spontaneous choice!" (no. 46). We can conclude from this, in response to some contemporary objections about the Church's alleged stubbornness in imposing celibacy on young men, that the authoritative Magisterium of Pius XI characterized it as the outcome of the free acceptance of a supernatural charism, which no one imposes or could impose. Rather the ecclesiastical norm must be understood as the decision by the Church to admit to the priesthood only those who have received the charism of celibacy and have freely accepted it.

Although it is legitimate to maintain that, in keeping with the mindset of its time, the basis for ecclesiastical celibacy in the encyclical *Ad Catholici Sacerdotii* by Pius XI is found in reasons, however valid, of ritual purity, nevertheless it is possible to recognize in that same document an important exemplary dimension, both in Christ's celibacy and in his freedom, which is the same freedom to which priests are called.

2. Pius XII and *Sacra Virginitas*

From the magisterial perspective, a decisive contribution was given by the encyclical *Sacra Virginitas* (March 25, 1954) by Venerable Pius XII. Like all the encyclicals of that pontificate, this one is splendid because of its clear, profound doctrinal basis and its wealth of biblical, historical, theological and spiritual references, and even today it is a remarkable, outstanding point of reference.

Although, strictly speaking the encyclical takes as its formal object not ecclesiastical celibacy but virginity for the kingdom of heaven, there are nevertheless in it a great many points for reflection and explicit references to the celibate state of the priesthood also.

The document is composed of four parts: the first delineates the "central idea of Christian virginity"; the second identifies and responds to some errors of the time, which are no less problematic even today; the third part describes the relation between virginity and sacrifice; while the last part, by way of conclusion, outlines some of the hopes and fears connected with virginity.

In the first part virginity is presented as an excellent way of living as a follower of Christ. "For what does following mean but imitation?" the pope asks. And he answers:

All these disciples and spouses of Christ embraced the state
of virginity.... It would hardly satisfy their burning love
for Christ to be united with Him by the bonds of affection, but this love had perforce to express itself by the imitation of His virtues, and especially by conformity to His
way of life, which was lived completely for the benefit and
salvation of the human race. If priests ... cultivate perfect
chastity, it is certainly for the reason that their Divine Master remained all His life a virgin. (no 19)

In reality, and certainly not by accident, the pope lik-
ens the priestly state of virginity to that of religious men
and women, thereby showing how celibacy, which is different from the normative point of view, in reality has
the same theological and spiritual foundation.

The pope identifies another reason for celibacy in the
need—which is connected to the mystery—for profound spiritual freedom. The encyclical declares: "It is
that they may acquire this spiritual liberty of body and
soul, and that they may be freed from temporal cares,
that the Latin Church demands of her sacred ministers
that they voluntarily oblige themselves to observe perfect chastity", and it adds: "Sacred ministers do not
renounce marriage solely on account of their apostolic
ministry, but also by reason of their service at the altar"
(nos. 22, 23). Thus it becomes evident that in the Magisterium of Pius XII the apostolic and missionary reason
is combined precisely with the cultic reason, in a synthesis that transcends all polarization and represents the
real and complete unity of the reasons in favor of priestly
celibacy.

Moreover in the apostolic exhortation *Menti Nostrae*,
the same Pius XII affirmed: "By this law of celibacy, the
priest not only does not abdicate his paternity, but increases
it immensely, for he begets not for an earthly and transitory

life but for the heavenly and eternal one" (in *Sacra Virginitas*, no. 26).

The missionary and sacred character of the minister, a realistic imitation of Christ, fruitfulness and spiritual fatherhood constitute therefore the indispensable parameters for priestly celibacy; incidentally, the document also corrects some errors that are still possible, such as the failure to recognize the objective excellence (and certainly not the subjective holiness) of the virginal state as compared with the married state, the assertion that it is humanly impossible to practice virginity or that consecrated persons are estranged from the life of the world and of society. In this regard the pope declares that souls consecrated to perfect chastity do not thereby impoverish their own human personality, since they receive from God himself spiritual assistance that is immensely more effective than the mutual help of spouses. In consecrating themselves directly to him who is their Principle and who communicates his Life to them, they are not impoverished but enriched (cf. no. 39).

These statements could suffice to respond with the necessary clarity to so many objections of a psychological or anthropological sort that are raised against priestly celibacy.

The last major and fundamental theme addressed by the encyclical *Sacra Virginitas* is the more specifically priestly theme of the relation between virginity and sacrifice. Citing Saint Ambrose, the pope remarks: "We are, therefore, merely invited by counsel to embrace perfect chastity, as something which can lead those 'to whom it is given' (Mt 19:11) more safely and successfully to the evangelical perfection they seek, and to the conquest of the kingdom of heaven. Wherefore it is 'not imposed, but proposed'" (no. 47). In this sense the invitation of Pius XII in the wake of the great Fathers of the Church is twofold: on the one hand, he affirms the duty to "gauge one's strength" so as to know whether one is capable of receiving the gift of grace that is celibacy, thus providing the whole Church, in this sense, especially in our time, with a sure criterion for honest discernment; on the other hand, he points out the intrinsic connection between chastity and martyrdom, teaching along with Saint Gregory the Great that chastity is a substitute for martyrdom and represents, in every age, the highest and most efficacious form of witness.

It is apparent to everyone how, especially in our secularized society, perfect continence for the kingdom of heaven is one of the more efficacious forms of witness that are capable of provoking the intellect and heart of our contemporaries in a salutary way. In a cultural climate that is increasingly and almost violently eroticized, chastity, especially the chastity of those in the Church on whom the ministerial priesthood has been conferred, is an even more powerfully eloquent challenge to the dominant culture that ultimately speaks to the very question about the existence of God and about the possibility of knowing him and entering into a relationship with him.

I feel that it is my duty now to highlight one final reflection on the encyclical by Pius XII, since this one, more than the others, appears to run decidedly contrary to many widespread customs today, even among some members of the clergy and in various programs of formation. Citing Saint Jerome, the pope points out how "for the preserving of chastity ... flight is more effective than open warfare.... Flight must be understood in this sense, that not only do we diligently avoid occasions of sin, but especially that in struggles of this kind we lift our minds and hearts to God, intent above all on Him to Whom we have vowed our virginity. 'Look upon the beauty of your Lover,' St. Augustine tells us" (no. 54).

Today it would seem almost impossible for an educator to transmit the value of celibacy and purity to young seminarians in a context wherein it proves in fact to be impossible to supervise their acquaintances or what they watch or read or view on the Internet. Although it is increasingly obvious and necessary to involve in a mature way the freedom of candidates in a voluntary, conscious collaboration in the work of formation, nonetheless the encyclical deems it a mistake, and we fully agree, to allow someone preparing for the priesthood to have any experience whatsoever, without the necessary discernment and the obligatory detachment from the world. To allow that is tantamount to understanding nothing about a man, his psychology or the society and culture that surround us. It means being shut up in a sort of preconceived ideology that runs contrary to reality. It is enough to look around. How much realism there is in the psalm verse: "They have eyes but see not"!

I must confess, at the end of this short *excursus* on the encyclical by Pius XII (and I could say the same about the one by Pius XI), that I am still surprised by its relevance to our own day. Although the main focus of both documents is on the sacral aspect of celibacy and on the connection between conducting worship and embracing virginity for the kingdom of heaven, the Magisterium of these two popes presents celibacy with a christological foundation, in its guidelines on the ontological configuration with Christ the Priest-Virgin and also in those concerning the imitation of Christ.

Many commentators see in the papal Magisterium on celibacy before the Second Vatican Council an insistence on sacral and ritual arguments, and in the Magisterium following the council an openness to more christological and pastoral reasons; this interpretation is in part justified.

Nevertheless it must be acknowledged—and this is fundamental for a correct hermeneutic of continuity, in other words, a Catholic hermeneutic—that both Pius XI and Pius XII extensively emphasize reasons of a theological nature. The above-mentioned pronouncements portray celibacy as being not only particularly opportune and appropriate for the priestly state, but also closely connected with the very essence of the priesthood, understood as a participation in the life of Christ, in his identity and therefore in his mission. Certainly it is no accident that the Eastern-rite churches that also ordain *viri probati* absolutely prohibit the admission of married priests to episcopal ordination!

3. John XXIII and *Sacerdotii Nostri Primordia*

As you know, Blessed John XXIII devoted an entire encyclical to the saintly Curé of Ars, on the first centennial of his birth to eternal life. In it the fundamental themes of virginity and celibacy for the kingdom of heaven, which were developed by Pope Pius XI and, above all, by Pope Pius XII, are adopted by John XXIII and, as it were, systematically applied to the exemplary figure of Saint John-Mary Vianney, whom he presents as the quintessence of the Catholic priesthood.

The pope points out how all the virtues that are necessary and proper for a priest had been acquired and practiced by Saint John-Mary Vianney, and in the text of the encyclical he lays the emphasis on priestly asceticism, the role of prayer and eucharistic devotion and the pastoral zeal that results from them.

Citing Pius XI, albeit indirectly, the encyclical acknowledges that, in order to carry out priestly duties, greater sanctity is needed than that required in the religious state, and he declares that the greatness of the priest consists in the imitation of Jesus Christ. John XXII affirms:

> The face of the Pastor of Ars shone with an angelic purity. And even now anyone who turns toward him in mind and spirit cannot help being struck, not merely by the great strength of soul with which this athlete of Christ reduced his body to slavery (cf. 1 Cor 9:27), but also by the great persuasive powers he exercised over the pious crowds of pilgrims who came to him and were drawn by his heavenly meekness to follow in his footsteps. (no. 24)

It becomes clear that, for Blessed John XXIII, the Curé of Ars gives splendid witness to the connection between ministerial effectiveness and fidelity to perfect continence for the kingdom of heaven and that this discipline is not defined in terms of the demands of the ministry but rather, contrary to any functionalistic reduction of the priesthood, the fullest flourishing of priestly ministry is defined and almost caused by fidelity to celibacy. The pope continues:

> The ascetic way of life, by which priestly chastity is preserved, does not enclose the priest's soul within the sterile confines of his own interests, but rather it makes him more eager and ready to relieve the needs of his brethren. St. John Mary Vianney has this pertinent comment to make in this regard: "A soul adorned with the virtue of chastity cannot help loving others; for it has discovered the source and font of love—God." (no. 25)

This perfectly theological argument makes it clear that the Spirit of God and the spirit of the world are diametrically opposed. Therefore we have the parameters necessary to grasp this idea and to develop it further.

The encyclical points out the essential connections between celibacy, priestly identity and the celebration of the divine mysteries. Particular emphasis is placed on the connection between the eucharistic offering of the divine Sacrifice and the daily gift of oneself, again in holy celibacy. Thus in 1959 the papal Magisterium already acknowledged that much of the confusion with respect to the faithful practice and the necessity of ecclesiastical celibacy depended and in fact depends on an insufficient understanding of its relation to the Eucharistic Celebration. Indeed, in that celebration the priest participates really, not just as a functionary, in the one, unrepeatable sacrifice of Christ, which, however, is sacramentally made present and re-presented in the Church for the salvation of the world. Such participation implies the offering of oneself, which must be total, including therefore also one's own flesh in virginity.

Who can miss then the vital connection between divine worship in the Eucharist and the ordained priesthood? The fate of worship is bound up with the fate of the priesthood. It is impossible to attend to one area without attending to the other. When someone accepts a position of responsibility in priestly formation he should reflect on and be aware of the fact that the fate of the new evangelization, which is absolutely indispensable, is bound up with the reform of the clergy.

The blessed pontiff notes, and it is still true today, perhaps even more dramatically: "We urge Our beloved priests to set aside a time to examine themselves on how they celebrate the divine mysteries, what their dispositions of soul and external attitude are as they ascend the altar and what fruit they are trying to gain from it" (no. 59). Thus the Eucharist is at the same time the source of sacred celibacy and a "test case" of fidelity to it, a concrete benchmark for the real offering of oneself to the Lord.

4. Paul VI and *Sacerdotalis Caelibatus*

Published on June 24, 1967, *Sacerdotalis Caelibatus* is the
last papal encyclical entirely devoted to the theme of celibacy. In the immediate aftermath of the council, while
accepting the conciliar teaching in its entirety, Paul VI
felt the need to reemphasize, with an authoritative magisterial act, the perennial validity of ecclesiastical celibacy, which, perhaps even more vehemently than today,
was being disputed in historical-biblical or theological-
pastoral studies that actually attempted to delegitimize it.

As is generally known, *Presbyterorum Ordinis* distin-
guishes between celibacy in itself and the law of celibacy,
in no. 16, where it says:

> Perfect and perpetual continence for the sake of the king-
> dom of heaven, commended by Christ the Lord and through
> the course of time as well as in our own days freely accepted
> and observed in a praiseworthy manner by many of the faith-
> ful, is held by the Church to be of great value in a special
> manner for the priestly life.... For these reasons, based on
> the mystery of Christ and his mission, celibacy, which first
> was recommended to priests, later in the Latin Church was
> imposed upon all who were to be promoted to sacred orders.

This distinction is found both in chapter 3 of the encyclical of Pius XI, *Ad Catholici Sacerdotii*, and also in no. 21
of the encyclical of Paul VI. Both documents still trace
the law of celibacy to its true origin, which is given by
the apostles and, through them, by Christ himself.

Servant of God Paul VI, in no. 14 of the encyclical,
declares:

> Hence We consider that the present law of celibacy should
> today continue to be linked to the ecclesiastical ministry.
> This law should support the minister in his exclusive,

definitive and total choice of the unique and supreme love
of Christ; it should uphold him in the entire dedication of
himself to the public worship of God and to the service of
the Church; it should distinguish his state of life both among
the faithful and in the world at large.

As is immediately evident, the pope adopts the cultic reasons specifically of the preceding Magisterium and inte-
grates them with the theological, spiritual and pastoral
reasons that were emphasized more by the Second Vatican Council, pointing out how these two kinds of reasons should never be considered antithetical but rather
complementary in a fruitful synthesis.

The same attitude can be found in no. 19 of the document, which recalls the duty of the priest as a minister
of Christ and a steward of the mysteries of God, an argument that culminates in a certain way in no. 21, which
declares:

Christ remained throughout His whole life in the state of
celibacy, which signified His total dedication to the service
of God and men. This deep [connection] between celibacy
and the priesthood of Christ is reflected in those whose for-
tune it is to share in the dignity and mission of the Mediator
and eternal Priest; this sharing will be more perfect the freer
the sacred minister is from the bonds of flesh and blood.

Wavering, therefore, in one's understanding of the inestimable value of sacred celibacy, and consequently in one's
proper appreciation for it and, when necessary, forceful
defense of it, could be interpreted as an inadequate understanding of the real import of the ordained ministry in
the Church and of its insuperable ontological-sacramental
and therefore real relation to Christ the High Priest.

The encyclical follows up these indispensable cultic and
christological references with a clear ecclesiological

reference that is also essential for a proper understanding of the value of celibacy:

> "Laid hold of by Christ" unto the complete abandonment of one's entire self to Him, the priest takes on a closer likeness to Christ, even in the love with which the eternal Priest has loved the Church His Body and offered Himself entirely for her sake, in order to make her a glorious, holy and immaculate Spouse. The consecrated celibacy of the sacred ministers actually manifests the virginal love of Christ for the Church, and the virginal and supernatural fecundity of this marriage, by which the children of God are born, "not of blood, nor of the will of the flesh." (no. 26)

How could Christ love his Church with a non-virginal love? How could the priest, an *alter Christus*, be spouse of the Church in a non-virginal way?

The overall argument of the encyclical shows the profound interconnectedness of all the values of sacred celibacy, which, from whatever side one may look at it, appears ever more radically and intimately connected with the priesthood.

Continuing to argue in support of celibacy based on ecclesiological reasons, the encyclical, in nos. 29, 30 and 31, points out the insuperable relation between celibacy and the Eucharistic Mystery, affirming that with celibacy

> the priest unites himself most intimately with the offering, and places on the altar his entire life, which bears the marks of the holocaust.... [B]y a daily dying to himself and by giving up the legitimate love of a family of his own for the love of Christ and of His kingdom, the priest will find the glory of an exceedingly rich and fruitful life in Christ, because like Him and in Him, he loves and dedicates himself to all the children of God.

The last major set of reasons that are presented in support of sacred celibacy concerns its eschatological significance. Celibacy acknowledges that the kingdom of God is not of this world (cf. Jn 18:36), that in the resurrection there will be neither marrying nor giving in marriage (cf. Mt 22:30) and that "the precious and almost divine gift of perfect continence for the kingdom of heaven stands out precisely as 'a special token of the rewards of heaven' (cf. 1 Cor 7:29–31)." Celibacy is described also as "a testimony to the ever-continuing progress of the People of God toward the final goal of their earthly pilgrimage, and as a stimulus for all to raise their eyes to the things above" (no. 34).

Anyone who had been placed in authority to guide the brethren to acknowledge Christ, to accept revealed truths and to lead an ever-more-blameless life—in a word, to holiness—thus finds in sacred celibacy a very fitting and extraordinarily forceful prophecy capable of conferring special authority on one's own ministry and both exemplary and apostolic fruitfulness to one's actions.

With extraordinary relevance, the encyclical also answers objections that would see in celibacy a mortification of human nature, thus deprived of one of the most beautiful aspects of life. The document declares in no. 56:

> In the priest's heart love is by no means extinct. His charity is drawn from the purest source, practiced in the imitation of God and Christ, and is no less demanding and real than any other genuine love. It gives the priest a limitless horizon, deepens and gives breadth to his sense of responsibility—a mark of mature personality—and inculcates in him, as a sign of a higher and greater fatherhood, a generosity and refinement of heart which offer a superlative enrichment.

In a word: "Celibacy sets the whole man on a higher level and makes an effective contribution to his perfection" (no. 55).

In 1967, the year in which the encyclical *Sacerdotalis Caelibatus* was published, Servant of God Paul VI performed one of the most courageous, exemplary and clarifying magisterial acts of his entire pontificate. This encyclical should be studied attentively by every candidate for the priesthood, from the beginning of his own formation, but certainly before submitting his request for admission to diaconal ordination; it should also be reviewed periodically in ongoing formation and made the object not only of careful biblical, historical, theological, spiritual and pastoral study, but also of in-depth, personal meditation.

5. John Paul II and *Pastores Dabo Vobis*

From the beginning of his pontificate, Servant of God John Paul II paid great attention to the theme of celibacy, stressing its perennial validity and pointing out the vital connection between it and the Eucharistic Mystery. On November 9, 1978, a few weeks after his election to the papal throne, in his first address to the clergy of Rome, he declared:

> The Second Vatican Council recalled to us this splendid truth regarding the "universal priesthood" of the whole People of God, which is derived from participation in the one priesthood of Jesus Christ. Our "ministerial" priesthood, rooted in the Sacrament of Holy Orders, differs essentially from the universal priesthood of the faithful.... Our priesthood must be clear and expressive, ... closely linked with celibacy, ... due precisely to the clarity and "evangelical"

expressiveness referred to in Our Lord's words on celibacy
"for the kingdom of heaven" (cf. Mt 19:12). (no. 3)

Certainly one particularly important document dealing with all the themes concerned with priesthood and
priestly formation was the apostolic exhortation *Pastores
Dabo Vobis*, in which the gift of celibacy is understood as
part of the bond between Jesus and the priest, and for
the first time, the psychological importance of this bond
is mentioned also in a way that is not separate from the
ontological importance. Indeed, we read in no. 72: "In
this bond between the Lord Jesus and the priest, an ontological and psychological bond, a sacramental and moral
bond, is the foundation and likewise the power for that
'life according to the Spirit' and that 'radicalism of the
Gospel' to which every priest is called today and which
is fostered by ongoing formation in its spiritual aspect."

Life according to the Spirit and the radicalism of the
gospel are therefore the two indispensable guidelines that
lead to a well-documented, cogent case for the lasting
validity of priestly celibacy. The fact that Servant of God
John Paul II immediately stresses its validity, proposes the
ontological-sacramental interpretation of it and goes so
far as to welcome the legitimate psychological implica-
tions that the charism of celibacy has in the formation of
a mature Christian and priestly personality encourages
and justifies the interpretation of this irreplaceable ecclesial treasure as a sign of the utmost uninterrupted continuity and, at the same time, as a bold form of prophecy.

We could indeed say that calling sacred celibacy into
question or relativizing it is a reaction contrary to the
promptings of the Spirit; whereas a full appreciation and
suitable acceptance of celibacy and its splendid, unsur-
passable witness constitute prophecy—true prophecy, even

in the Church today, even though she is burdened by recent tragedies that have horribly defiled her white robe, and even more obviously in contrast with hyper-eroticized societies in which the trivialization of sexuality and corporeality reigns supreme.

The celibate shouts to the world that God exists, that he is love and that it is possible in every era to live totally by him and for him. And it is completely natural that the Church should choose her priests from among those who have maturely accepted pro-existence—being for an Other, for Christ!—and brought it to such a high level, which is therefore prophetic.

The Magisterium of John Paul II, which so attentively appreciates both the family and the role of women in the Church and in society, has no fear whatsoever of repeating the perennial validity of sacred celibacy. Quite a few studies are now being conducted on the interesting and enormously consequential theme of corporeality and the theology of the body in the thought of Pope John Paul II.

The very same pontiff, who perhaps more than others in recent times elaborated and lived out this great theology of the body, also commends to us a radical love for celibacy and, through his explanation of the ontological-sacramental and theological-spiritual dimensions of it, invites us to overcome any attempt to reduce it to merely functionalistic terms.

One final element that emerges—not an innovation so much as an invaluable emphasis—in the Magisterium of John Paul II (and already present in *Presbyterorum Ordinis*) is the element of priestly fraternity. It is not interpreted reductively in psychological-emotional terms, but rather with respect to its sacramental root, both in relation to holy orders and in regard to the presbyterate united with their own bishop. Priestly fraternity is a constitutive part of ordained ministry, bringing to light the "bodily" dimension thereof. It is the natural place for those healthy fraternal relations of practical assistance, both material and spiritual, and of companionship and support along the common path of personal sanctification through the ministry that is entrusted to us.

I want to make one final reference to the *Catechism of the Catholic Church*, which was published during the pontificate of John Paul II in 1992. It is, as many emphasize, the authentic tool available to us for a correct interpretation of the documents of the Second Vatican Council. And it is increasingly evident that it is sure to become the indispensable point of reference both for catechesis and for all apostolic action. The *Catechism* authoritatively reiterates the perennial validity of priestly celibacy in paragraph 1579:

> All the ordained ministers of the Latin Church, with the exception of permanent deacons, are normally chosen from among men of faith who live a celibate life and who intend to remain *celibate* "for the sake of the kingdom of heaven" (Mt 19:12). Called to consecrate themselves with undivided heart to the Lord and to "the affairs of the Lord" (1 Cor. 7:32), they give themselves entirely to God and to men. Celibacy is a sign of this new life to the service of which the Church's minister is consecrated; accepted with a joyous heart celibacy radiantly proclaims the Reign of God.

All the themes touched on thus far by the papal Magisterium, which we have just examined, are marvelously condensed in the definition in the *Catechism*—from the cultic reasons to those concerning the imitation of Christ in proclaiming the kingdom of God, from those derived from apostolic service to the ecclesiological and eschatological reasons. The fact that the reality of celibacy made it into the *Catechism of the Catholic Church* indicates how closely connected it is with the heart of the Christian faith; it is a witness to the splendid proclamation that the same text speaks about.

6. Benedict XVI and *Sacramentum Caritatis*

The last pope we will examine is the happily reigning Benedict XVI, whose initial magisterial teaching on priestly celibacy leaves no doubt whatsoever either about the perennial validity of the disciplinary norm or, prior to that and most importantly, about its theological and in particular christological, eucharistic foundation.

Indeed the Holy Father dedicated to the theme of celibacy an entire paragraph of the post-synodal apostolic exhortation *Sacramentum Caritatis*:

> The Synod Fathers wished to emphasize that the ministerial priesthood, through ordination, calls for complete configuration to Christ. While respecting the different practice and tradition of the Eastern Churches, there is a need to reaffirm the profound meaning of priestly celibacy, which is rightly considered a priceless treasure, and is also confirmed by the Eastern practice of choosing Bishops only from the ranks of the celibate. These Churches also greatly esteem the decision of many priests to embrace celibacy. This choice on the part of the priest expresses in a special way the dedication which conforms him to Christ and his exclusive offering of himself for the Kingdom of God. The fact that Christ himself, the eternal Priest, lived his mission even to the sacrifice of the Cross in the state of virginity constitutes the sure point of reference for understanding the meaning of the tradition of the Latin Church. It is not

sufficient to understand priestly celibacy in purely functional terms. Celibacy is really a special way of conforming
oneself to Christ's own way of life. This choice has first
and foremost a nuptial meaning; it is a profound identification with the heart of Christ the Bridegroom who gives
his life for his Bride. In continuity with the great ecclesial
tradition, with the Second Vatican Council and with my
predecessors in the papacy, I reaffirm the beauty and the
importance of a priestly life lived in celibacy as a sign express-
ing total and exclusive devotion to Christ, to the Church
and to the kingdom of God, and I therefore confirm that it
remains obligatory in the Latin tradition. Priestly celibacy
lived with maturity, joy and dedication is an immense blessing for the Church and for society itself. (no. 24)

It is easy to see that the apostolic exhortation reiterates the invitation to priests to lead a life of self-offering,
even unto the sacrifice of the cross, through total and
exclusive dedication to Christ. Particularly significant is
the connection, stressed by the apostolic exhortation,
between celibacy and the Eucharist; if this theology of
the Magisterium is received genuinely and is really applied
in the Church, the future of celibacy will be splendid
and fruitful, because it will be a future of priestly freedom and holiness. Thus we could speak not only about
the "nuptial meaning" of celibacy, but also about its
"eucharistic meaning", derived from the offering that
Christ perennially makes of himself to the Church, which
is reflected in an obvious way in the life of priests. They
are called to reproduce, in their own lives, the sacrifice
of Christ, to whom they have been assimilated by virtue
of priestly ordination.

From the eucharistic meaning of celibacy proceed all
the possible theological developments of it, which confront the priest with his own fundamental duty: the

celebration of Holy Mass, in which the words: "This is my Body" and "This is my Blood" not only define the sacramental effect that is proper to them, but gradually and really should shape the offering of priestly life itself.

The celibate priest is thus personally and publicly associated with Jesus Christ; he makes him really present, becoming himself a victim in what Benedict XVI calls "the Eucharistic logic of Christian life".

The more the centrality of the Eucharist, worthily celebrated and perpetually adored, is recovered in the life of the Church, the greater will be the fidelity to celibacy and the understanding of its inestimable value and, if I may say so, the flourishing of holy vocations to the ordained ministry.

In his *Address to the Roman Curia for the Exchange of Christmas Greetings*, on December 22, 2006, Benedict XVI also declared:

> The true foundation of celibacy can be contained in the phrase: *Dominus pars*—You are my land. It can only be theo-centric. It cannot mean being deprived of love, but must mean letting oneself be consumed by passion for God and subsequently, thanks to a more intimate way of being with him, to serve men and women, too. Celibacy must be a witness to faith: faith in God materializes in that form of life which only has meaning if it is based on God. Basing my life on him, renouncing marriage and the family, means that I accept and experience God as a reality and that I can therefore bring him to men and women.

Only the experience that the Lord himself is the inheritance, the portion, for every priestly life makes celibacy effective as a witness to the faith. As the same Holy Father emphasized to the Plenary Assembly of the Congregation for the Clergy on March 16, 2009, this *apostolica vivendi forma* "consists in participation in a 'new life', spiritually speaking, in that 'new way of life' which the Lord Jesus inaugurated and which the Apostles made their own."

During the recently concluded Year for Priests, the Holy Father gave several talks on the theme of priesthood, particularly in his Wednesday catecheses dedicated to the *tria munera* [three offices, i.e., governing, teaching, sanctifying], in his talks on the occasion of the inauguration and conclusion of the Year for Priests and on the anniversaries connected with Saint John-Mary Vianney. Particularly relevant was the Holy Father's dialogue with priests at the close of the Year for Priests. When asked about the significance of celibacy and about the troubles encountered in practicing it in contemporary culture, he began his reply by noting the centrality of daily celebration of the Eucharist in the life of a priest: acting *in persona Christi*, the priest speaks in the "I" of Christ, thus becoming a concrete instance of the perpetuation of Christ's unique priesthood in time. The pope added: "This unification of his 'I' with ours implies that we are 'drawn' also into the reality of his Resurrection; we are going forth towards the full life of resurrection. . . . In this sense, celibacy is anticipation. We transcend this time and move on. By doing so, we 'draw' ourselves and our time towards the world of the resurrection, towards the newness of Christ, towards a new and true life." Thus the Magisterium of Benedict XVI has sanctioned the close relation between the eucharistic dimension of priestly celibacy, which makes it a source of priestly life and ministry, and its eschatological dimension, whereby it anticipates and realizes something of the world to come. Overcoming in one stroke all functionalistic, reductive views of priestly ministry, the Holy Father places it within its full, lofty theological context, illumines it by pointing out its constitutive relation with the Church as a consequence thereof and forcefully appreciates all the missionary power resulting precisely from this "something more" for the sake of the kingdom of God that celibacy embodies.

On that same occasion, with prophetic boldness, the Holy Father declared: "For the agnostic world, the world in which God does not enter, celibacy is a great scandal, because it shows exactly that God is considered and experienced as reality. With the eschatological dimension of celibacy, the future world of God enters into the reality of our time."

How could the Church live without the scandal of celibacy? Without men who are ready to affirm the reality of God in the present, even and, above all, through their own flesh? These affirmations found their fulfillment and, so to speak, their crowning in the extraordinary homily given at the close of the Year for Priests—which I take the liberty of inviting you to reread—in which the pope prayed that, as the Church, we might be freed from lesser scandals so that the true scandal of history, which is Christ the Lord, might appear.

Conclusions

At the end of this review, in which we have pointed out some of the more important passages of the papal Magisterium on celibacy, from Pius XI to Benedict XVI, let us try to draw some initial conclusions that can serve as the primary basis in the formation of priests to accept and live out fully this gift from the Lord.

1. What is evident, first of all, is the radical continuity between the Magisterium that preceded the Second Vatican Council and the Magisterium subsequent to it.

Although there are sometimes remarkably different emphases, more liturgical-sacral or more christological-pastoral, the uninterrupted Magisterium of the aforementioned pontiffs is consistent in basing celibacy on the theological reality of the ministerial priesthood, on the ontological-sacramental configuration of the priest to Christ the Lord, on his participation in his Christ's unique priesthood and on the *imitatio Christi* that that implies. Only a superficial interpretation of the council documents could lead someone to regard celibacy as a remnant from the past from which the Church should free herself as quickly as possible. Such a position, besides being historically, doctrinally and theologically erroneous, is also extremely harmful from a spiritual, pastoral, missionary and vocational perspective.

2. In light of the papal Magisterium that has been examined, the reduction of celibacy to a mere ecclesiastical law, which is so widespread in some circles, must be overcome. It is a law only because it is an intrinsic requirement of the priesthood and of the configuration to Christ intended by the sacrament of holy orders.

In this sense formation for celibacy, over and above any other human or spiritual consideration, must include a solid doctrinal component, since one cannot practice something without understanding the reason for it.

3. The debate over celibacy that has periodically been rekindled over the centuries does not foster an intellectual climate in which younger generations can understand such a decisive factor in priestly life. Everyone should take to heart what was authoritatively expressed in *Pastores Dabo Vobis*, which in paragraph 29 reports verbatim the intention of the entire Synod Assembly:

> The Synod does not wish to leave any doubts in the mind of anyone regarding the Church's firm will to maintain the

law that demands perpetual and freely chosen celibacy for present and future candidates for priestly ordination in the Latin rite. The Synod would like to see celibacy presented and explained in the fullness of its biblical, theological and spiritual richness, as a precious gift given by God to his Church and as a sign of the kingdom which is not of this world—a sign of God's love for this world and of the undivided love of the priest for God and for God's people.

4. Celibacy is a question of evangelical radicalism. Poverty, chastity and obedience are not counsels reserved exclusively for consecrated religious; they are virtues to practice with an intense missionary passion. We cannot betray our young men. We cannot lower the level of formation and, *de facto*, of our proclamation of the faith. We cannot betray the holy people of God, which expects holy pastors like the Curé of Ars. We must be radical in following Christ. And we do not fear a shortage of clerics. The number decreases when the ardor of the faith diminishes, because vocations are not of human but of divine origin and follow the divine logic, which is human folly. What is needed is faith.

5. In a seriously secularized world, it is increasingly difficult to understand the reasons for celibacy. Nevertheless, we must have the courage, as a Church, to ask ourselves whether we intend to resign ourselves to this situation, accepting as an inevitable fact the progressive secularization of societies and cultures, or whether we are ready for the work of a real and profound new evangelization, in the service of the gospel and therefore of the truth about man.

Along these lines, I maintain that well-motivated support for celibacy and adequate appreciation for it in the life of the Church and of the world can be some of the most efficacious means of overcoming secularization.

Otherwise what else would Holy Father Benedict XVI mean when he declares that celibacy "shows exactly that God is considered and experienced as reality".

6. The theological root of celibacy is to be traced back to the new identity that is given to the man on whom the order of priesthood is conferred. The centrality of the ontological-sacramental dimension of the priesthood and its resulting eucharistic foundation are the framework within which celibacy is naturally understood, promoted and faithfully lived out. The essential question then is not to be found so much in the debate over celibacy as in the quality of the faith in our communities. If a community did not have great esteem for celibacy, how could its life reflect an expectation of the kingdom of God or a longing for the Eucharist?

7. I am convinced that knowledge of the foundations of celibacy and the joyous experience of living it out fully, which is therefore profoundly humanizing, allow a priest not only to respond to all the challenges that the world poses to celibacy, but also to transform celibacy into a challenge to the world. As mentioned in the first of these conclusions, we must not allow ourselves to be influenced or intimidated by a world without God, which does not comprehend celibacy and would like to eliminate it, but on the contrary, we must recover the well-founded awareness that our celibacy challenges the world, sending its secularism and its agnosticism into a profound crisis and crying out through the ages that God exists and is present!

Appendix

Appendix

Excerpts from Other Significant Magisterial Documents on Priestly Celibacy

Selected by Arturo Cattaneo and Manfred Hauke

Documents from Christian antiquity

The oldest legislative document, reflecting previous tradition, is offered by the Council of Elvira, in southern Spain (circa 306). Here is the central statement: "We have decreed a general prohibition for married bishops, priests and deacons, or also for all clerics who have been appointed to the ministry: they must not come together with their wives and they must not beget children. Whosoever shall do the same shall be expelled from the ranks of the clergy" (canon 33).

The situation in the Church during the early centuries presents no particular differences between East and West, as various testimonies demonstrate; this is made clear particularly by those of Saint Epiphanius, Bishop of Salamina, of Saint Jerome, one of the great Fathers of the Western Church, and of the Emperor Justinian.

In the fourth century, several synods in the West stressed the apostolic origin of continence for bishops, priests and deacons. Among them are the Roman Synod of 386 and the North African Synod of 390. The Synod of Rome, together with the decree by Pope Siricius *Cum in unum*, underscores that it is necessary to hold fast to

the precepts "that have been neglected because of igno-
rance and sloth" of some—precepts that "go back to
the apostles and were established by the Fathers" regarding chastity. It is

> worthy, chaste, and honest that the priests and Levites have
> no intercourse with their wives, for the clergy are occupied
> with the daily duties of their ministries. Paul, writing to
> the Corinthians, says: "Abstain from one another so as to
> be free for prayer" (1 Cor 7:5). If continence is com-
> manded for lay people so that their prayers may be heard,
> how much more must the priest be ready at any moment,
> in perfect purity and confidence, to offer sacrifice or to
> baptize?

Another important contribution is made by the Council of Carthage (390). It took place within the context
of a battle between Donatists and Catholics (the
Donatists denied the validity of sacraments conferred by
clerics who were considered unworthy). Each party
pointed to the moral failings of the clerics of the other.
The protocol of the council informs us that the assembly referred to an earlier council (which had strictly confirmed the chastity of bishops, priests and deacons) and
to the apostolic teaching on the abstinence of sacred
ministers (i.e., bishops, priests and deacons) from the
beginning.

One of the bishops said: "What the apostles taught
and what antiquity itself observed, let us also endeavor
to keep." ("Quod apostoli docuerunt et ipsa servavit antiq-
uitas, nos quoque custodiamus.") Then the bishops
declared unanimously: "It pleases us all that bishops, priests,
and deacons, guardians of purity, abstain from conjugal
intercourse with their wives, so that those who serve at
the altar may keep a perfect chastity."

Documents from the Middle Ages

The ancient Church expected bishops, priests and deacons to practice continence even if they happened to be married. This discipline underwent a development in the Middle Ages, in the West, arriving at the precept of celibacy in the stricter sense: only unmarried men or at least married men who were not living together with their wives were admitted to holy orders.

The tenth century, called by some historians the Iron Century, was characterized by a considerable cultural and religious decline, which led to a widespread abandonment of the practice of celibacy among the clergy. The Gregorian reform in the eleventh century promoted a resumption of the discipline, which was then sanctioned by the First Lateran Council in 1123. The Second Lateran Council, in 1139, further added the particular ruling that marriage contracted after ordination is declared null. We reprint one of the principal statements:

> We absolutely forbid priests, deacons, or subdeacons the intimacy of concubines and of wives, and cohabitation with other women, except those with whom for reasons of necessity alone the Nicene Synod [First Council of Nicaea, in 325, canon 3] permits them to live, that is, a mother, sister, paternal or maternal aunt, or others of this kind concerning whom no suspicion may justly arise. (Lateran Council I, canon 3)

Documents from the Council of Trent to Vatican II

Luther maintained that it was impossible to take a vow of chastity. Given this challenge, the Council of Trent reiterated the possibility of taking such a vow and defined the greater dignity of the state of virginity, following the teaching of Saint Paul, who emphasizes that virginity for love of Christ is "better" than marriage (cf. 1 Cor 7:25–40).

During the Enlightenment era, celibacy was opposed, as it was also in the period of modernism, against which Pope Pius X decisively responded in his encyclical *Pascendi* (1907).

All the popes of the twentieth century defended priestly celibacy. The most important documents before Vatican II are the apostolic exhortation *Haerent Animo* by Pius X (1908), the 1917 Code of Canon Law (canons 132 and 1072), the encyclical *Ad Catholici Sacerdotii* by Pius XI (1935) and the encyclical *Sacra Virginitas* by Pius XII (1954). We cite here several important excerpts from the two encyclicals.

> A priest's charge is to be solicitous for the eternal salvation of souls, continuing in their regard the work of the Redeemer. Is it not, then, fitting that he keep himself free from the cares of a family, which would absorb a great part of his energies? ... Notwithstanding all this, We do not wish that what We said in commendation of clerical celibacy should be interpreted as though it were Our mind in any way to blame, or, as it were, disapprove the different discipline legitimately prevailing in the Oriental Church. What We have said has been meant solely to exalt in the Lord something We consider one of the purest glories of the Catholic priesthood; something which seems to us to correspond better to the desires of the Sacred Heart of Jesus and to His purposes in regard to priestly souls. (*Ad Catholici Sacerdotii*, nos. 45 and 47, in *Acta Apostolicae Sedis*, 28, 1936)

While speaking about consecrated virginity, Pius XII paid special attention also to the celibacy of sacred ministers:

Or rather does not the Apostle Paul admit that they have the right of abstaining for a time from the use of marriage, so that they may be more free for prayer (cf. 1 Cor 7:5), precisely because such abstinence gives greater freedom to the soul which wishes to give itself over to spiritual thoughts and prayer to God?

Finally, it may not be asserted, as some do, that the "mutual help" which is sought in Christian Marriage is a more effective aid in striving for personal sanctity than the solitude of the heart, as they term it, of virgins and celibates. For although all those who have embraced a life of perfect chastity have deprived themselves of the expression of human love permitted in the married state, nonetheless it cannot thereby be affirmed that because of this privation they have diminished and despoiled the human personality. For they receive from the Giver of heavenly gifts something spiritual which far exceeds that "mutual help" which husband and wife confer on each other. They consecrate themselves to Him Who is their source, and Who shares with them His divine life, and thus personality suffers no loss, but gains immensely. For who, more than the virgin, can apply to himself that marvelous phrase of the Apostle Paul: "I live, now not I; but Christ liveth in me" (Gal 2:20)?

For this reason the Church has most wisely held that the celibacy of her priests must be retained; she knows it is and will be a source of spiritual graces by which they will be ever more closely united with God. (*Sacra Virginitas*, nos. 38–40, in *Acta Apostolicae Sedis*, 46, 1954)

Vatican Council II, *Optatam Totius* (1965)

10. Students who follow the venerable tradition of celibacy according to the holy and fixed laws of their own rite are to be educated to this state with great care. For renouncing thereby the companionship of marriage for

the sake of the kingdom of heaven (cf. Mt 19:12), they embrace the Lord with an undivided love altogether befitting the new covenant, bear witness to the resurrection of the world to come (cf. Lk 20:36), and obtain a most suitable aid for the continual exercise of that perfect charity whereby they can become all things to all men in their priestly ministry. Let them deeply realize how gratefully that state ought to be received, not, indeed, only as commanded by ecclesiastical law, but as a precious gift of God for which they should humbly pray. Through the inspiration and help of the grace of the Holy Spirit let them freely and generously hasten to respond to this gift.

Students ... are to be warned of the dangers that threaten their chastity especially in present-day society. Aided by suitable safeguards, both divine and human, let them learn to integrate their renunciation of marriage in such a way that they may not only suffer no harm from celibacy in their lives and work but rather acquire a deeper mastery of soul and body and a fuller maturity, and more perfectly receive the blessedness spoken of in the Gospel.

Vatican Council II, *Presbyterorum Ordinis* (1965)

Celibacy is to be embraced and esteemed as a gift:

16. Perfect and perpetual continence for the sake of the kingdom of heaven, commended by Christ the Lord and through the course of time as well as in our own days freely accepted and observed in a praiseworthy manner by many of the faithful, is held by the Church to be of great value in a special manner for the priestly life. It is at the same time a sign and a stimulus for pastoral charity and a special source of spiritual fecundity in the world. Indeed, it is not demanded by the very nature of

the priesthood, as is apparent from the practice of the early Church and from the traditions of the Eastern Churches, where, besides those who with all the bishops, by a gift of grace, choose to observe celibacy, there are also married priests of highest merit. This holy synod, while it commends ecclesiastical celibacy, in no way intends to alter that different discipline which legitimately flourishes in the Eastern Churches. It permanently exhorts all those who have received the priesthood and marriage to persevere in their holy vocation so that they may fully and generously continue to expend themselves for the sake of the flock commended to them.

Indeed, celibacy has a many-faceted suitability for the priesthood. For the whole priestly mission is dedicated to the service of a new humanity which Christ, the victor over death, has aroused through his Spirit in the world and which has its origin "not of blood, nor of the will of the flesh, nor of the will of man but of God" (Jn 1:13). Through virginity, then, or celibacy observed for the kingdom of heaven, priests are consecrated to Christ by a new and exceptional reason. They adhere to him more easily with an undivided heart, they dedicate themselves more freely in him and through him to the service of God and men, and they more expeditiously minister to his kingdom and the work of heavenly regeneration, and thus they are apt to accept, in a broad sense, paternity in Christ. In this way they profess themselves before men as willing to be dedicated to the office committed to them—namely, to commit themselves faithfully to one man and to show themselves as a chaste virgin for Christ and thus to evoke the mysterious marriage established by Christ, and fully to be manifested in the future, in which the Church has Christ as her only Spouse. They give, moreover, a living sign of the world to come, by a faith and charity already made present, in which the children of the resurrection neither marry nor take wives.

For these reasons, based on the mystery of Christ and his mission, celibacy, which first was recommended to priests, later in the Latin Church was imposed upon all who were to be promoted to sacred orders. This legislation, pertaining to those who are destined for the priesthood, this holy synod again approves and confirms, fully trusting this gift of the Spirit so fitting for the priesthood of the New Testament, freely given by the Father, provided that those who participate in the priesthood of Christ through the sacrament of Orders—and also the whole Church—humbly and fervently pray for it. This sacred synod also exhorts all priests who, in following the example of Christ, freely receive sacred celibacy as a grace of God, that they magnanimously and wholeheartedly adhere to it, and that persevering faithfully in it, they may acknowledge this outstanding gift of the Father which is so openly praised and extolled by the Lord. Let them keep before their eyes the great mysteries signified by it and fulfilled in it. Insofar as perfect continence is thought by many men to be impossible in our times, to that extent priests should all the more humbly and steadfastly pray with the Church for that grace of fidelity, which is never denied those who seek it, and use all the supernatural and natural aids available. They should especially seek, lest they omit them, the ascetical norms which have been proved by the experience of the Church and which are scarcely less necessary in the contemporary world. This holy synod asks not only priests but all the faithful that they might receive this precious gift of priestly celibacy in their hearts and ask of God that he will always bestow this gift upon his Church.

Other magisterial documents since Vatican II

Congregation for Catholic Education, *A Guide to Formation in Priestly Celibacy* (1974)

31. *Emotional maturity in the priest:*

The choice of priestly celibacy does not interfere with the normal development of a person's emotional life, but, on the contrary, it presupposes it. A celibate is called to express his ability to love in a special way. Having grown up in human and divine love, a priest can responsibly decide the manner in which he will, for his whole life, form his emotional relationships.

Celibacy chosen "for the sake of the kingdom of heaven" is the celibacy proper to the priest. It is falling in love. It is possible only for someone who has integrated it into his spiritual life. It is a matter of choosing exclusively, perpetually, and completely the unique and supreme love of Christ for the purpose of more deeply sharing his lot by the resplendent and heroic logic of a singular and unlimited love for Christ the Lord and for His Church.

By virtue of his celibacy, a priest becomes more totally a man of God. He lets himself be more completely taken over by Christ, and lives only for Him. Virginal love invited him to possess God in a fuller way, to reflect Him and give Him to others in His fullness.

The love that a priest has for others must be essentially pastoral in aim. Externally it should be shown by a warm-heartedness which is indispensable in disposing people to accept the spiritual support a priest offers them.

A priest can form true and profound friendships. These are particularly useful to his emotional development when they are fostered within the priestly fraternity.

32. *Sexual maturity in the priest:*

Celibacy, as a personal option made for a higher good, even one completely on the natural level, can result in a fully mature and integrated personality. This can be even more true when celibacy is chosen for the kingdom of heaven, as can be seen in the lives of many saints and faithful, who dedicate themselves in a celibate life to the service of God and man, promoting human and Christian progress.

The exclusive nature of a candidate's choice of priestly celibacy, when he becomes a special possession of God, determines also his duties and particular dedication to the love of God in Christ. One who chooses virginity in virtue of his determination to give himself exclusively to sharing in the priesthood of Christ is obliged to grow in love of God and his neighbor. If he does not progress in this love, he is not following his vocation.

There is something sublime in the qualities roused in a man's heart by natural fatherhood: an altruistic spirit, the assumption of heavy responsibilities, a capacity for love and a dedication enough to make any sacrifice, daily bearing of life's burdens and difficulties, prudent care for the future, etc. However, all this is equally true of spiritual paternity. Moreover, spiritual fatherhood, not being confined to the natural order, is even more responsible and heroic.

For this reason, celibacy is not for everyone. Celibacy requires a special vocation from the Lord. Throughout the whole of life, it is never without risk and danger, since something can always occur to take the heart out of a man's universal and pastoral fatherhood and his exclusive dedication to Christ.

33. *Self-control of the priest:*

Continuous self-control implies constant effort. This is necessary not only to acquire emotional maturity, but also for persevering in it. Ongoing self-control impedes regression from emotional adulthood once this is attained. It is an irreplaceable factor in the practice of human, Christian, and priestly chastity, which should always be able to check any new or unforeseen resurgence of emotional stimulation.

In the Christian view of continuous and progressive self-control, priestly celibacy appears as a lifelong offering to our Lord. To be consecrated in holy celibacy is not simply a single action made once at ordination. It is rather something that has to be renewed again and again, in the constant vigilance a priest must exercise when faced with human attraction and the emotions and passion of affection and love.

Just as with natural human love, the fullness of love which is involved in celibacy requires the daily practice of glad self-renunciation. This is the only way to conquer the difficulties that, with the passage of time, can come from boredom or from the weakness of the flesh.

A priest should always find an incentive for self-control in the thought that the personal sacrifice demanded by his celibacy is serving the whole Church. His sacrifice underlines the spiritual dimension that must mark all love worthy of the name, and it merits grace for Christian families.

38. *Evaluating the authenticity of a vocation:*

One remarkably important educational goal, in relation to the whole problem of education for celibacy, is to help the young man become aware of his own inclinations and his own abilities to overcome possible difficulties connected with the celibate state. And if ever he should find out that he does not have the necessary qualities, he needs to act in a way that is capable of making the proper vocational choice conscientiously, courageously and with commitment. The errors in discerning vocations are not rare, and in all too many cases psychological defects, sometimes of a pathological kind, reveal themselves only after ordination to the priesthood. Detecting defects earlier would help avoid many tragic experiences.... The selection of candidates is a difficult and at the same time a delicate thing; it requires true commitment on the part of all the educators to prepare for it and to carry it out. It should be done according to the criteria of a suitable diagnostic investigation, which is possible today through the science of psychology, and must take into account, along with the supernatural factor, many human prerequisites. It can be safely assumed that well-prepared educators are capable of verifying the authenticity of vocations in normal individuals, with the usual criteria for selection. In particular cases, or whenever it seems appropriate to those responsible for seminary education, so as to be of more assistance to the individual candidates in discerning their own vocation, it will be opportune—and sometimes even necessary—to have recourse to specific remedies: the psychological examination of the candidate before he begins the theology curriculum; specialized counseling, even of a psychotherapeutic nature; the interruption of ecclesiastical studies so as to gain experience in professional work.

Congregation for the Clergy, *Directory on the Ministry and Life of Priests* (1994)

59. *Example of Jesus.*

Celibacy, then, is a gift of self "in" and "with" Christ to his Church and expresses the service of the priest to the Church "in" and "with" the Lord.

It would be entirely immature to see celibacy as "a tribute to be paid to the Lord" in order to receive Holy Orders rather than "a gift received through his mercy", as the free and welcomed choice of a particular vocation of love for God and others.

The example is Christ, who in going against what could be considered the dominant culture of his time, freely chose to live celibacy. In following him the disciples left "everything" to fulfil the mission entrusted to them (Lk 18:28–30).

For this reason the Church, from apostolic times, has wished to conserve the gift of perpetual continence of the clergy and choose the candidates for Holy Orders from among the celibate faithful (cf. 2 Thess 2:15; 1 Cor 7:5; 9:5; 1 Tim 3:2–12; 5:9; Tit 1:6–8).

Congregation for Bishops, *Directory for the Ministry of Bishops* Apostolorum successores (2004)

82. *Attentiveness to Clerical Celibacy.*

In order to help priests maintain a chaste commitment to God and to the Church, the Bishop needs to take great care that celibacy is presented in all its Biblical, theological and spiritual richness. He should encourage all his priests to lead a profound spiritual life and to seek divine assistance, so that their hearts may be filled with love for Christ.

The Bishop should strengthen the bonds of fraternity and friendship between priests, and should take pains to show the positive value that exterior solitude can have for their interior life and for their human and priestly maturity. He should present himself to them as a faithful friend and confidant, to whom they may entrust themselves in search of understanding and good counsel.

The Bishop should be aware of the *real obstacles* which, today more than in the past, stand in the way of priestly celibacy. He should therefore exhort his priests to practise supernatural and human prudence, teaching them that being proper and discreet in their comportment towards women is in accord with their consecrated celibacy, whereas greater familiarity, if misinterpreted, could lead to sentimental attachment. If necessary, he should intervene to warn anyone who might be putting himself at risk. Depending on the circumstances, the Bishop may wish to establish concrete norms in order to facilitate the observance of the promises associated with priestly ordination

Benedict XVI, *Address to the Roman Curia for the Exchange of Christmas Greetings* (December 22, 2006)

Paul calls Timothy—and in him, the Bishop and in general the priest "man of God" (I Tim 6:11). This is the central task of the priest: to bring God to men and women. Of course, he can only do this if he himself comes from God, if he lives *with* and *by* God. This is marvellously expressed in a verse of a priestly Psalm that we—the older generation—spoke during our admittance to the clerical state: "The Lord is my chosen portion and my cup, you hold my lot" (Ps 16[15]:5). The priest praying in this Psalm interprets his life on the basis of the distribution of territory as established in Deuteronomy (cf. 10:9). After taking possession of the Land, every tribe obtained by the drawing of lots his portion of the Holy Land and with this took part in the gift promised to the forefather Abraham. The tribe of Levi alone received no land: its land was God himself. This affirmation certainly had an entirely practical significance.

Priests did not live like the other tribes by cultivating the earth, but on offerings. However, the affirmation goes deeper. The true foundation of the priest's life, the ground of his existence, the ground of his life, is God himself. The Church in this Old Testament interpretation of the priestly life—an interpretation that also emerges repeatedly in Psalm 119[118]—has rightly seen in the following of the Apostles, in communion with Jesus himself, as the explanation of what the priestly mission means. The priest can and must also say today, with the Levite: *"Dominus pars hereditatis meae et calicis mei"*. God himself is my portion of land, the external and internal foundation of my existence. This theocentricity of the priestly existence is truly necessary in our entirely function-oriented world in which everything is based on calculable and ascertainable performance. The priest must truly know God from within and thus bring him to men and women: this is the prime service that contemporary humanity needs. If this centrality of God in a priest's life is lost, little by little the zeal in his actions is lost. In an excess of external things the centre that gives meaning to all things and leads them back to unity is missing. There, the foundation of life, the "earth" upon which all this can stand and prosper, is missing.

Celibacy, in force for Bishops throughout the Eastern and Western Church and, according to a tradition that dates back to an epoch close to that of the Apostles, for priests in general in the Latin Church, can only be understood and lived if [it] is based on this basic structure. The solely pragmatic reasons, the reference to greater availability, are not enough: such a greater availability of time could easily become also a form of egoism that saves a person from the sacrifices and efforts demanded by the reciprocal acceptance and forbearance in matrimony; thus, it could lead to a spiritual impoverishment or to hardening of the heart. The true foundation of celibacy can be contained in the phrase: *Dominus pars*—You are my land. It can only be theocentric. It cannot mean being deprived of love, but must mean letting oneself be consumed by passion for God and subsequently, thanks to a more intimate way of being with him, to serve men and women, too.

Celibacy must be a witness to faith: faith in God materializes in that form of life which only has meaning if it is based on God. Basing my life on him, renouncing marriage and the family, means that I accept and experience God as a reality and that I can therefore bring him to men and women. Our world, which has become totally positivistic, in which God appears at best as a hypothesis but not as a concrete reality, needs to rest on God in the most concrete and radical way possible. It needs a witness to God that lies in the decision to welcome God as a land where one finds one's own existence. For this reason, celibacy is so important today, in our contemporary world, even if its fulfilment in our age is constantly threatened and questioned.

A careful preparation during the journey towards this goal and persevering guidance on the part of the Bishop, priest friends and lay people who sustain this priestly witness together, is essential. We need prayer that invokes God without respite as the Living God and relies on him in times of confusion as well as in times of joy. Consequently, as opposed to the cultural trend that seeks to convince us that we are not capable of making such decisions, this witness can be lived and in this way, in our world, can reinstate God as reality.

Congregation for Catholic Education, *Guidelines in the Use of Psychology in the Admission and Formation of Candidates for the Priesthood* (2008)

2. Some of these qualities merit particular attention: the positive and stable sense of one's masculine identity, and the capacity to form relations in a mature way with individuals and groups of people; a solid sense of belonging, which is the basis of future communion with the presbyterium and of a responsible collaboration in the ministry of the bishop; the freedom to be enthused by great ideals and a coherence in realizing them in everyday action; the courage to take decisions and to stay faithful to them; a knowledge of oneself, of one's talents and limitations, so as to integrate them within a self-esteem before God; the capacity to correct oneself; the appreciation for beauty in the sense of "splendour of the truth" as well as the art of recognizing it; the trust that is born from an esteem of the other person and that leads to acceptance; the capacity of the candidate to integrate his sexuality in accordance with the Christian vision, including in consideration of the obligation of celibacy.[1]

Such interior dispositions must be moulded during the future priest's path of formation because, as a man of God and of the Church, he is called to build up the ecclesial community. Being in love with Him who is Eternal, the priest develops an authentic and integral

---

[1] Paul VI, in his Encyclical Letter *Sacerdotalis Caelibatus*, deals explicitly of this necessary capacity of the candidate for the priesthood, in nn. 63–63: *AAS* 59 (1967), 682–683. In n. 64, he concludes: "The life of the celibate priest, which engages the whole man so totally and so delicately, excludes in fact those of insufficient physical, psychic and moral qualifications. Nor should anyone pretend that grace supplies for the defects of nature in such a man." Cf. also *Pastores Dabo Vobis*, n. 44: *AAS* 84 (1992), 733–736.

appreciation of humanity. He also increasingly lives the richness of his own affectivity in the gift of himself to God, One and Three, and to his brethren, particularly those who are suffering.

Clearly, these are objectives that can only be reached by the candidate co-operating daily with the work of grace within him. They are objectives that are acquired with a gradual and lengthy path of formation, which is not always linear.[2]

8. When evaluating whether it is possible for the candidate to live the charism of celibacy in faithfulness and joy, as a total gift of his life in the image of Christ the Head and Shepherd of the Church, let it be remembered that it is not enough to be sure that he is capable of abstaining from genital activity. It is also necessary to evaluate his sexual orientation, according to the indications published by this Congregation.[3] Chastity for the kingdom, in fact, is much more than the simple lack of sexual relationships.

[2] In the developing formation process, affective maturity takes on a particular importance; this is an area of development that requires, today more than ever, particular attention. "In reality, we grow in affective maturity when our hearts adhere to God. Christ needs priests who are mature, virile, capable of cultivating an authentic spiritual paternity. For this to happen, priests need to be honest with themselves, open with their spiritual director and trusting in divine mercy" (Benedict XVI, Speech to priests and religious in the Cathedral of Warsaw [25 May 2006], in L'Osservatore Romano [26–27 May 2006], p. 7). Cf. Pontifical Work for Ecclesiastical Vocations, New Vocations for a New Europe, Final Document of the Congress on Vocations to the Priesthood and to the Consecrated Life in Europe, Rome, 5–10 May 1997, published by the Congregations for Catholic Education, for the Oriental Churches, for Institutes of Consecrated Life and Societies of Apostolic Life (6 January 1998), n. 37.

[3] Cf. Congregation for Catholic Education, Instruction concerning the Criteria for the Discernment of Vocations with regard to Persons with Homosexual Tendencies in View of Their Admission to the Seminary and to Holy Orders (4 November 2005): AAS 97 (2005), 1007–1013.

Benedict XVI, *Address to Participants in the Conference Organized by the Congregation for the Clergy* (March 12, 2010)

Dear brother priests, in the time in which we live it is particularly important that the call to participate in the one Priesthood of Christ in the ordained Ministry flourishes in the "charism of prophecy": there is a great need for priests who speak of God to the world and who present God to the world; men who are not swayed by transient cultural trends but are capable of living authentically that freedom which alone the certainty of belonging to God can give. As your Convention has clearly emphasized, the most necessary prophecy today is that of faithfulness, which, based on Christ's Faithfulness to humanity, leads through the Church and the ministerial Priesthood to living one's own priesthood in total adherence to Christ and to the Church. Indeed, the priest no longer belongs to himself but, because of the sacramental seal he has received (cf. *Catechism of the Catholic Church*, nn. 1563, 1582), is the "property" of God. The priest's "belonging to Another", must become recognizable to all, through a transparent witness.

In the way of thinking, speaking, and judging events of the world, of serving and loving, of relating to people, also in his habits, the priest must draw prophetic power from his sacramental belonging, from his profound being. Consequently he must do all he can to separate himself from the predominant mindset that tends not to associate the minister's value with his being but with his function alone, thereby underestimating the work of God, which affects the profound identity of the priest as a person, configuring him to himself once and for all (cf. ibid., n. 1583).

The horizon of the ontological belonging to God also constitutes the proper framework for understanding and reaffirming, in our day too, the value of sacred celibacy which in the Latin Church is a charism required for Sacred Orders (cf. *Presbyterorum Ordinis*, no. 16) and is held in very great consideration in the Eastern Churches (cf. CCEO, can. 373). It is an authentic prophecy of the kingdom, a sign of consecration with undivided heart to the Lord and to "the affairs of the Lord" (1 Cor 7:32), the expression of their gift of self to God and to others (cf. *Catechism of the Catholic Church*, n. 1579).

Bibliography

ANATRELLA, T. "Quelques enjeux psychologiques du célibat sacerdotale". *Revue d'éthique et de théologie morale, Supplément,* 196 (1996): 47–60.

BALLETTA, R. AND A. MARDEGAN, EDS. *Sacerdozio e celibato nella Chiesa.* Milan: Edizioni Centro Ambrosiano, 2007.

BECKER, KLAUS M. AND JÜRGEN EBERLE. *Der Zölibat des Priesters.* Sankt Ottilien: EOS Verlag, 1995.

CHOLIJ, R. *Clerical Celibacy in East and West.* Leominster, UK: Fowler Wright Books, 1988.

COCHINI, C. *Origines apostoliques du célibat sacerdotal.* Paris-Namur: Lethielleux, 1981; second edition Geneva: Ad Solem, 2006. English translation: *Apostolic Origins of Priestly Celibacy.* San Francisco: Ignatius Press, 1990.

COPPENS, J., ED. *Sacerdozio e celibato: Studi storici e teologici.* Milan: Edizioni Ancora, 1975. Original French edition: *Sacerdoce et célibat: Études historiques et théologiques.* Gembloux/Louvain: Duculot, 1971.

COZZENS, D. *The Changing Face of the Priesthood.* Collegeville, Minnesota: The Liturgical Press, 2000.

———. *Sacred Silence: Denial and the Crisis in the Church.* Collegeville, Minnesota: The Liturgical Press, 2004.

HAUKE, M. "La connessione tra sacerdozio ministeriale e celibato". In *Il sacerdozio ministeriale: "l'amore del Cuore di Gesù"*, edited by S. M. Manelli and S. M. Lanzetta. Frigento: Casa Mariana Editrice, 2010.

HEID, S. *Zölibat in der frühen Kirche: die Anfänge einer Enthalt-samkeitspflicht für Kleriker in Ost und West.* Paderborn: Schöningh, 1997, 2003. English translation: *Celibacy in the Early Church: The Beginnings of a Discipline of Oblig-atory Continence for Clerics in East and West.* San Francisco: Ignatius Press, 2000. Polish translation: *Celibat w Kosciele pierwotnym: Poczatki obowiazku wstrzemiezli-wosci dla duchownych na Wschodzie i na Zachodzie.* Tuchów: Mała Poligrafia, 2000.

HOHMANN, J. S. *Der Zölibat: Geschichte und Gegenwart eines umstrittenen Gesetzes mit einem Anhang wichtiger kirchli-cher Quellentexte.* Frankfurt am Main: Lang, 1993.

LA POTTERIE, I. DE. "Il fondamento biblico del celibato sacerdotale". In *Solo per amore: Riflessioni sul celibato sac-erdotale,* edited by I. de la Potterie et al. Introduction by Cardinal José T. Sánchez. Cinisello Balsamo: Ediz-ioni Paoline, 1993.

LA POTTERIE, I. DE ET AL., EDS. *Solo per amore: rif-lessioni sul celibato sacerdotale.* Introduction by Cardinal José T. Sánchez. Cinisello Balsamo: Edizioni Paoline, 1993.

LORDA, J. L., ED. *El celibato sacerdotal: espiritualidad, disci-plina y formación de las vocaciones al sacerdocio.* Pamplona: Edizioni EUNSA, 2006.

MARINI, M. *Celibato sacerdotale: apostolica vivendi forma.* Siena: Cantagalli, 2005.

MARZOTTO, D. *Celibato Sacerdotale e Celibato di Gesù.* Casale Monferrato: Piemme, 1987.

MCGOVERN, T. *Priestly Celibacy Today.* Princeton: Scep-ter; Dublin: Four Courts Press; Chicago: Midwest Theo-logical Forum, 1998. Spanish translation: *El celibato sacerdotal: una perspectiva actual.* Madrid: Cristiandad, 2004.

METTLER, P. *Die Berufung zum Amt im Konfliktfeld von Eig-nung und Neigung: Eine Studie aus pastoraltheologischer und kirchenrechtlicher Perspektive, ob Homosexualität ein objektives Weihehindernis ist.* Frankfurt am Main: Peter Lang, 2008.

————. "Unbequeme Wahrheiten—warum Homosexualität ein objektives Weihehindernis ist". *Forum Katholische Theologie* 25 (2009): 110–138.

ROCCHETTA, C. "Riflessioni teologiche sulla reciprocità matrimonio-verginità". In *Verginità e matrimonio: Due parabole dell'Unico Amore,* edited by R. Bonetti, 73–101. Milan: Edizioni Ancora, 1998.

STICKLER, A. M. *Der Klerikerzölibat: Seine Entwicklungsgeschichte und seine theologischen Grundlagen.* Abensberg: Kral-Verlag, 1993. Italian translation: *Il celibato ecclesiastico: La sua storia e i suoi fondamenti teologici.* Città del Vaticano: Libreria Editrice Vaticana, 1994. English translation: *The Case for Clerical Celibacy: Its Historical Development and Theological Foundation.* San Francisco: Ignatius Press, 1995.

TOUZE, L., *L'avenir du célibat sacerdotal et sa logique sacramentelle.* Paris: Parole et Silence/Lethielleux, 2009.

Contributors

Adè, Édouard: Instructor at the Catholic University of West Africa (Côte d'Ivoire), priest.

Anaya, Luis Alfredo: Instructor at the Seminary of the Archdiocese of Paraná and the Higher Institute of Philosophy and Religious Sciences "Fons Vitae" (Argentina), priest.

Cattaneo, Arturo: Instructor on the Canon Law faculty of Saint Pius X (Venice) and the Theology faculty in Lugano (Switzerland), priest.

Charamsa, Krzysztof: Official of the Congregation for the Doctrine of the Faith, instructor with the Theology faculty of the Pontifical Athenaeum Regina Apostolorum (Rome) and the Theology faculty of the Pontifical Gregorian University (Rome), priest.

Ejeh, Benedict: Instructor on the Canon Law faculty of Saint Pius X (Venice), former Secretary of the Juridical Committee of the Bishops Conference of Nigeria, priest.

Gefaell, Pablo: Instructor of Eastern Canon Law at the Pontifical University of the Holy Cross ("Santa Croce", Rome), Consultor for the Pontifical Council for the Interpretation of Legislative Texts, priest.

Hauke, Manfred: Instructor on the Theology faculty of Lugano (Switzerland), priest.

Heid, Stefan: Instructor at the Pontifical Institute of Christian Archaeology (Rome), priest.

Jerumanis, André-Marie: Instructor on the Theology faculty in Lugano (Switzerland), priest and physician.

Kochappilly, Paulachan: Instructor at the Pontifical Athenaeum of Philosophy, Theology and Canon Law (Dharmaram Vidya Kshetram, Bangalore, India), priest.

Lütz, Manfred: Doctor of medicine (psychiatry) and head physician at a clinic in Bonn (Germany), member of the Pontifical Council for the Laity and consultor of the Congregation for the Clergy.

Malnati, Ettore: Instructor on the faculty of Political Sciences of the University of Trieste and the Theology faculty of Lugano (Switzerland), priest and pastor.

Manzi, Franco: Instructor at the Archdiocesan Seminary of Milan, the Theology faculty of Northern Italy, the Higher Institute for Religious Sciences in Milan and the Theology faculty of Lugano (Switzerland), priest.

Mettler, Peter: Instructor at the *Instituto Santo Tomás de Aquino* (ISTA) in Belo Horizonte (Brazil), judge of the tribunal of the Archdiocese of Belo Horizonte, priest.

Paximadi, Giorgio: Instructor on the Theology faculty of Lugano (Switzerland), priest.

Schwarz, Johannes Maria: Instructor at the International Theological Institute of Trumau (Vienna), priest.

Volonté, Ernesto William: Instructor on the Theology faculty of Lugano (Switzerland) and the Catholic University of Milan, rector of St. Charles Borromeo Diocesan Seminary (Lugano), priest.